Bill Oddie's
INTRODUCTION TO
BIRDWATCHING

This edition published in 2013 by New Holland Publishers (UK) Ltd
London • Cape Town • Sydney • Auckland
www.newhollandpublishers.com

10 9 8 7 6 5 4 3 2 1

Garfield House, 86–88 Edgware Road, London W2 2EA, UK
Wembley Square, Solan Road Gardens, Cape Town 8001, South Africa
1/66 Gibbes Street, Chatswood, NSW 2067, Australia
218 Lake Road, Northcote, Auckland, New Zealand

First published in 2002 by New Holland Publishers (UK) Ltd
Copyright © 2013, 2002 in text: Bill Oddie
Copyright © 2013, 2002 in photographs: David M. Cottridge
 and other photographers as credited below
Copyright © 2013, 2002 in artwork: New Holland Publishers (UK) Ltd
Copyright © 2013, 2002 New Holland Publishers (UK) Ltd

A CIP catalogue record for this book is available from the British Library.

ISBN 978 1 78009 410 6

Publisher: Simon Papps
Project Editors: Lorna Sharrock, Mike Unwin
Copy Editor: Sylvia Sullivan
Artwork: David Daly.
Designer: Rosamund Saunders
Index: Janet Dudley
Production: Joan Woodroffe
Printer: Toppan Leefung Printing Ltd (China)

All photography by David M. Cottridge, with the exception of the following (t= top; b=bottom;
c=centre; l=left; r=right): Rene H. de Heer (Windrush Photos) p49(l); Mike Wilkes p59(t,b);
Chris Gomersall p78; Roger Wilmshurst pp88, 91; Tom Ennis p120; David Kjaer pp126, 131;
Chris Packham p130; Simon Papps pp12, 24, 25, 29 (t,b), 30, 31 (t,b), 32, 33b, 34, 62, 63, 103.

Also available

Bill Oddie's Birds of Britain and Ireland (2nd edition): £12.99, ISBN 978 1 78009 245 4

Bill Oddie's Birding Map: £4.99, ISBN 978 1 84 773 981 0

Follow New Holland Publishers on
Facebook: www.facebook.com/NewHollandPublishers

Bill Oddie's

INTRODUCTION TO
BIRDWATCHING

SECOND EDITION

NEW
HOLLAND

THE
wildlife
TRUSTS

THE WILDLIFE TRUSTS

There are 47 Wildlife Trusts across the UK, as well as the Isle of Man and Alderney, all working towards a collective vision of 'an environment rich in wildlife for everyone'. With more than 800,000 members, 150,000 of which belong to our junior branch Wildlife Watch, we are the largest UK voluntary organisation dedicated to conserving the UK's full range of species and habitats.

We have a mission to create Living Landscapes and secure Living Seas, restoring and reconnecting habitats for a tomorrow where our countryside and cities are richer in wildlife than they are today. Together we manage more than 2,300 nature reserves and each year advise thousands of land owners on improving landscapes and habitats for nature. Our advocacy and campaigning work also ensures that a wide range of policies and decisions reflect the importance of our natural environment.

The Wildlife Trusts have been described as the UK's leading provider of access to nature. We want to inspire people about the natural world so that they value it, understand their relationship with it and take action to protect and restore it. Each year we engage directly with more than 600,000 people, including schoolchildren and students,

bringing wildlife to the classroom or the classroom outdoors. We also welcome more than 7 million visitors to our nature reserves annually and run hundreds of walks, events and activities, including birdwatching trips, dawn chorus walks and a huge range of others.

Bill Oddie is Vice President of The Wildlife Trusts. In his *Introduction to Birdwatching* you can discover some of the thrills of the natural world. Bill introduces us to the simple joys of watching and listening for birds like Song Thrush, Skylark or Blackcap, and for the more adventurous and patient the rare boom of the Bittern or the haunting cry of the Manx Shearwater. But you don't need to visit nature reserves to experience birds for yourself. While many birders choose to explore every corner of the British Isles, for many the local park or back garden can provide a good starting point and be just as enjoyable.

The work we do would not be possible without the support of our members, volunteers and partners. To find out more about The Wildlife Trusts, support our work by joining or take part in an event near you, call 01636 677711 or visit www.wildlifetrusts.org

The Wildlife Trusts is a registered charity (number 207238).

CONTENTS

INTRODUCTION

It is customary for books like this one to start with a rave about how wonderful – beautiful, fascinating, entertaining, important – birds are. I'm not going to do that. I'm going to assume you think that anyway. I'm also going to assume that you are thinking of becoming a 'real' birdwatcher. Well, my initial response to that is simply: "Yes. Go on, do it!"

I'm not going to analyze the appeal of birdwatching, but all I will say is that it has kept me intrigued, busy, happy and arguably sane for 60 years. It is quite simply a hobby for a lifetime. And I'm not the only one who thinks that. There are literally millions of birdwatchers all over the world and the number is growing daily.

I quote the editorial I was reading in the "business" magazine on a transatlantic flight recently (yes, that's how bored I got!) which stated: "Birding is the biggest growth leisure pursuit in the western world." That's marketing speak for "it's getting more and more popular!" So you'll be in good company.

Or will you? What exactly is a real birdwatcher? As opposed to someone who just enjoys watching birds. An audience analysis of my BBC series "Birding With Bill Oddie" concluded that about 90 per cent of my viewers "would not consider themselves real birdwatchers". Is that modesty, or embarrassment? I sometimes wonder if it is the latter. Let's face it, there are certain cliché images and stereotypes of the "typical birdwatcher", and maybe you don't fancy being labelled accordingly. I've heard them, us – including me – labelled

as "anoraks". I presume this implies that birdwatchers are rather boring, narrow-minded, and ramble on tediously about birds and nothing much else. Well, of course there are bird bores, but then there are bores in just about every area. As for literally wearing an anorak … very sensible, I'd say! If you are outdoors in all kinds of weather, it's just as well to wear some protective clothing. Added to which, I thought anoraks and woolly hats were rather hip these days – street cred gear, in fact.

But there really is no such thing as the typical birdwatcher. I honestly believe there can be very few other leisure pursuits that attract such a wide spectrum of types of people as birdwatching. I have met all kinds: millionaire businessmen, clergy, punks, hippies, young, old, all races and religions, and both sexes, and variations in between, all unified by their passion for birds. Indeed, I would go as far as to say that birdwatching is fantastic for bringing people together. Believe me, birders are all very different under their anoraks!

The other cliché image of modern birdwatching is of "twitchers". In fact, the media have hijacked this word and often use it to refer to any level of birdwatching. I once appeared in a photo in a national newspaper along with Julian Pettifer and a bunch of youngsters who had designed a bird garden. We were all labelled as "twitchers", simply because the project had something to do with birds. Wrong! Twitching is in fact a specialized, specific and indeed rather extreme kind of birdwatching. It is first and foremost the pursuit of rarities.

THE TRUE MEANING OF TWITCHING

It is also invariably "mass" birding, when large crowds travel from far and wide and gather to tick off one – often small, dull, but rare – bird. Not surprisingly, this sort of thing appeals to the media no end. The image of ranks and ranks of almost identical-looking bearded blokes with thousands of pounds worth of optical gear does undeniably make for an eye-catching photo in the paper, or "jokey"

Above: *Time was when you could identify a 'real birdwatcher' by his or her ownership of a telescope and a tripod. Not any more! They've all got them now.*

Above: *In fact, these people are breaking one of the basic birding rules: don't suddenly appear over the horizon. No doubt they were in pursuit of something really rare, and got over-excited. Now they've probably scared it away.*

item at the end of the news. And if the behaviour of the twitchers gets a bit frantic, so much the better. Maybe the bird flies over the hill and the hordes race off in pursuit, or it flies off altogether and the late arrivals miss it and are reduced – sometimes literally – to tears. It happens. The emotions involved in twitching can be pretty extreme. In fact, that's where the word comes from. It was coined many many years ago among a then small group of rarity chasers, some of whom would get so over excited at the prospect of seeing a new bird, or so frantically nervous that they might miss it, that they would literally shake, palpitate or "twitch" with the emotion of the whole thing. It is certainly true that

twitching can be stressful. It can also be expensive and time consuming. It is also pretty much male dominated. I can entirely appreciate that this all adds up to an image that puts off quite a number of people who may be considering becoming birdwatchers. Well, let me reassure you on several points. First and foremost, twitching is not "normal birdwatching", even if the media may mislead you into thinking it is. Secondly, as it happens, twitching can also be great fun. But thirdly – and most importantly – you don't have to go twitching at all to be a birdwatcher. In fact, if you are relatively new to birds, I'd go so far as to say that you shouldn't really go twitching … yet. (See chapter 9).

IT'S WHATEVER YOU WANT IT TO BE

I hope I have convinced you that you don't have to conform to some cliché image. The truly splendid thing about birdwatching is that you really can enjoy it on whatever level you want. So, in a sense perhaps, there is no such thing as a "real" birdwatcher. There are, of course, let's call them, differing levels of ability. There are scientific ornithologists, field craft experts, people who know quite a bit, and people who know very little. However, I really do not believe that there is anybody that knows nothing at all about birds. Here's another reason to be encouraged: you may feel that you are a complete beginner, but I bet you know more than you realize.

I am convinced that everyone has some small basic knowledge of and probably interest in birds. At the very least, we all notice them – they are surely the most conspicuous form of wildlife, be they pigeons in the park, Robins in the garden, or "sea gulls" on the beach. We are also introduced to them at a very early age. There can't be many of us who as toddlers – or even as babies in prams – weren't taken to feed the ducks. I recall that I and my then-toddling grandson used to visit the duck pond on Hampstead Heath near where I live in London. I call it a "duck

Below: *Feeding the ducks: many people's first contact with birds. They may behave as if they are tame (the ducks I mean), but the chances are that many of them are wild.*

pond", but of course the wildfowl that came for our crusts weren't just ducks. There were Canada Geese and Mute Swans, and Coots and Moorhens. What's more, within minutes my grandson realized this (and not just because I told him.) "That's a swan, isn't it, Grandad?" "Yes." "And that's a Canada Goose." That one surprised me, until I remembered that one of his babysitters was Canadian! "And what's that?" he asked, pointing at a Coot. He didn't know its name, but he knew it was something different. Now, I'm not saying he would become a birdwatcher, but he was already watching birds, and he was already beginning to identify them.

We counted the different species we could see on the pond, and it came to nearly a dozen. I repeat, non-birders know more than they think. Even when they are only toddlers.

The same principle applies to garden birds. I have had people say to me, "Oh, I never get any birds in my garden (or back yard) and anyway, they all look the same to me." It's never true. "Think about it. How about Starlings, Blackbird, Robin, Blue and Great Tits, Wood Pigeon, Wren, Magpie?" "Oh, yes I know those." So there we are, that person knows more than they thought or realized. Everyone does.

Below: *"They all look the same." I think not! Ironically, the one that you may know best – the House Sparrow – is becoming worryingly scarce. The other two are Great Tit and Chaffinch.*

TO SUM UP

Don't be put off by cliché images. Don't be worried that you won't be able to identify birds. Get involved on whatever level you want. Be encouraged by what you already know, and by the fact that there are birds everywhere, nearby, wherever you live.

Try a little test … Look out of your window at the garden – or beyond – for maybe half an hour, or – better still – go for a stroll in the local park, or in the countryside, if that's where you live. As you are looking or walking, be conscious of how many birds you recognize, and how many birds you don't recognize. Look in different areas: on the lawn, in the bushes, in the tree tops, on water, and in the sky. Notice how certain birds prefer different habitats. And listen. Listen for bird song and bird calls. Don't worry that you can't identify them yet. But do be conscious of them. Notice the differences. You are already developing bird "awareness". The basis of birdwatching. If you don't see or hear that much, don't be put off. Birds move around, and the bird population of the same area can change quite a bit from day to day, season to season and place to place. Sadly, it is true that some species may be getting scarcer – though others are getting commoner – but in any event, take my word for it, there is still plenty to see and to enjoy.

As a matter of fact, non-birders have quite frequently – and I suspect usually with a touch of derision – asked me: "So, what do you actually do when you go birdwatching? Sit in a hide all day, up to your knees in mud?" My answer is: "Well, I have done that, but 90 per cent of the time it's just being out there, walking and noticing what you see as you go along." And anyone can do that.

Left: *Can there be anybody in Britain or Ireland who wouldn't recognize a Robin? So that's one you've identified for starters.*

LOOKING IT UP

I am convinced that everyone likes to put a name to a bird. Whenever I go for a walk on Hampstead Heath, non-birders come up to me and ask "what's that bird?" or they tell me "I've just seen a bird I don't recognize, what is it?" Sometimes they describe it and I can put a name to it for them. Often I'm convinced that they must have seen the species before, but have only just noticed them. "What are those big black birds on the rafts on the pond?" "They're Cormorants." "Really? I've never seen them before." I have to resist saying "I bet you have. They are there every day in winter." I suppose what makes a potential birdwatcher is being aware of birds, noticing the differences between families and species, and becoming mildly obsessed with wanting to put a name to them. "Identification" is the word for it. And the essential book for you is a field guide.

Your initial task, though, is identifying a field guide! The first rule about seeking out bird books – any kind of bird books – is to go to a specialist dealer. Sadly, many normal book shops (even the big ones) often have a very poor selection in the natural history department. So it is worth seeking out a specialist shop, or mail ordering after browsing through a catalogue. I'll say this now and I'll be saying it again: birdwatching is so popular nowadays that a whole industry has grown up to service it. Books, optical equipment, outdoor clothing, CDs, DVDs, Apps, specialist holidays. Whatever the birdwatcher requires or desires is available from people who understand your needs. So please don't go somewhere that doesn't! There really is no excuse for making a bad choice. All these companies advertise in the various bird and wildlife magazines (see page 137) and online.

WHAT *IS* A FIELD GUIDE?

So, back to books. There are lots of bird books that aren't field guides. They may be – like this one – about birdwatching, or about bird behaviour, or maybe just a nice selection of bird pictures. Technically, the "guide" bit means a guide to identification. The "field" bit implies that the book is small enough to slip in a pocket or rucksack and take out "in the field", so you can look up birds on the spot. This is useful, but not essential. Ironically, I suspect that many birdwatchers would consider that it is an indication of their expertise if they don't carry a field guide. It isn't simply that they don't need to. There is, in fact, a lot to be said for seeing a bird in the field, making notes and looking it up in the book later (see page 50). The detective process helps to make it stick. There are many excellent field guides, and the standard of modern art work is extremely high. Tastes vary and different birdwatchers have different favourite books, but – let's be honest – there are a few that consistently get "top marks", mainly because the illustrations are truly exceptional.

CHOOSING THE RIGHT ONE

There are a few basic criteria that should be met when choosing a field guide. If you are birding in the United Kingdom, the book should contain all the species that occur regularly in the British Isles. Each species should be shown in a variety of plumages: male, female, summer, winter and juveniles. Many birds should be shown both at rest and in flight. Some species need five or six

Above and right: *Many species have several different plumages. A good guide will show them all. A breeding adult Black-headed Gull (foreground, standing, and top centre, flying) looks entirely different from the first winter (top left, flying) and first summer (top right, standing).*

pictures to truly represent them. Since there are over 200 relatively common British birds, it stands to reason that there are going to be an awful lot of pictures and pages. To cram them all in the book may get pretty bulky, or the pictures may get small or cramped. OK, a tiny book may seem attractively portable, but does it contain enough species, or are the illustrations too small to be really clear?

REMEMBER YOU'RE BRITISH!

One thing I am beginning to feel very strongly about. Many – perhaps most – field guides – and this includes some unarguable masterpieces – cover Britain and Europe. This may seem great value, but … Well, let me tell you a story. Last summer I decided to get into the identification of dragonflies, butterflies and moths. I had a very basic knowledge, but when I went out into the field I soon realized that I was very much a beginner. Nevertheless, my birdwatching had taught me to take notes and do little sketches, and this I did. Then, when I got home, I looked them up in the books, only to find myself faced with pages and pages of apparently almost identical insects. I was totally overwhelmed, and somewhat discouraged, until it struck me that my butterfly and dragonfly guides both covered Britain and Europe. In fact, when I started reading the text I realized that the vast percentage of the illustrations were of species that never occurred in Britain at all. I began sifting through them, eliminating most, and attempted to work out what I was most likely to have seen, but it was a tedious and irritating process. So, I went out and

bought two more books, British Butterflies and Moths, and Dragonflies of Britain and Ireland, since when I have found the whole thing a lot easier, and indeed more satisfying, not least because I soon realized I'd already seen a fair percentage of the commoner species! As it happens, there are a lot more kinds of birds in Britain than either butterflies or dragonflies, and probably a greater percentage of them do occur across the Channel as well. Nevertheless, I really do recommend starting off with a British Isles only field guide (and I'm not just saying that because I happen to have written one!)

Another excellent feature of my butterfly book is that it has a section at the back for rarities. This is also a very good idea for birds. One of the crucial rules of birding (not only for beginners actually!) is that if you see a bird you don't recognize, it is still probably NOT a rarity. Rarities are rare, but if they are included in the main part of a field guide people start seeing them! So, another feature to check on before you buy your book: rarities either at the back, or carrying a clear warning sign in the text alongside the pictures. Eventually, you may – or probably will – travel in Europe, or simply become a more advanced birder. That's the time to buy yourself one of the truly great field guides, because they really are wonderful. Buy one now if you can afford it, or are curious, or confident that you are going to need it eventually, but – take my advice – in the early days, stick to the common birds.

A few field guides are illustrated with photographs rather than paintings. Logically, one might assume that photos would be more realistic and therefore more helpful, but I don't believe this is the case (and I think most birders agree with me). I suppose it is because a good artist can show you exactly what you need to know: each species in all plumages, posed to show off all its features, in perfect light, with no distracting background. Photographs may be more natural, but the very naturalism – a distorted pose, shadows, or the orange effect of sunlight – can actually make the species less easily recognized. Added to which, even the most prolific photographic library probably hasn't got a slide of every British bird in every plumage. Having said

Below: Rarities are rare! Your chances of finding one are very small. But don't worry: although some are worth seeing, many of them look really boring.

that, there are some photographic guides that are extremely thorough and very pleasing. By all means buy one, for aesthetic reasons if nothing else, and as an extension to your illustrated guides, but if you asked me to choose between artwork and photos, I'd have to say artwork.

OK, so you've decided which guide you want to buy, or maybe you have already got it. You flick through it. A couple of things that may boggle you a bit: most guides begin with what look like bird anatomy charts, on which all sorts of feather areas are marked, all labelled with almost unpronounceable Latin type words. The whole thing is probably headed "Bird Topography", which could be a euphemism for "instant turn off"! Glance at the diagrams if you like. You

Below left and opposite above: *Willow Warbler.*
Ironically, an illustration will often show a more
quintessentially accurate image than does a
photograph (no disrespect to photographers).
Also – be honest – there is something aesthetically
pleasing about beautiful bird paintings (still no
disrespect to photographers!).

Below and opposite below: *Common Chiffchaff. There*
are some stunning photos too. Fortunately, these two
warblers - which, let's face it, look almost identical -
have completely different songs. So that's the easiest
way to tell them apart. Even pretty-experienced birders
sometimes refer to them as 'willow/chiffs', unless the
birds are singing.

may well come to understand them, even use them in the future. One day you may start chatting about "supercilia" and "tertials", but – for the moment – do yourself a favour: *ignore them!* The fact that the book starts with the topography page almost implies that you need to study and absorb it in order to identify the birds that follow in the rest of the book. *You don't!* Phew! That's a relief, isn't it?

Moving on to the rest of the field guide, you may still be a bit intimidated by the sheer number of species: over 200, plus all those rarities at the back. A bit overwhelming? There are only about 30 common British butterflies and even fewer

dragonflies. Yes, but you only see them in summer, and they really aren't as easy to see as birds, and more birds means more variety, and … trust me! Here is a little exercise to give you confidence. Look through your field guide and be aware – and be encouraged – by how many species you do recognize. Even when you get to pages of ones that all look the same, say to yourself: "Well yes, but I do know it's some kind of goose, or duck, or gull, or wader." You will soon realize that most similar-looking birds are at least in the same group or family. And as it happens, whichever guide you buy, you will find that these families are also in the same order in the book. (It is all to do

Left: *A female Reed Bunting with all its bits and pieces named. But you don't need to know a single one of them to recognize it.*

FOREHEAD
CROWN
EAR-COVERTS
BILL
NAPE
THROAT
MANTLE
BREAST
LESSER COVERTS
BACK
MEDIAN COVERTS
TERTIALS
SCAPULARS
GREATER COVERTS
RUMP
ALULA
UPPERTAIL-COVERTS
VENT
FLANK
SECONDARIES
BELLY
PRIMARY COVERTS
UNDERTAIL-COVERTS
PRIMARIES
TAIL

Above: *At a distance, these two could look very similar, but one is a gull and the other is a wader. It's obvious, if you can see the bills.*

with scientific classification. You don't really need to know. I don't!) Towards the end of the book, you will find more and more pages of "little brown jobs", and yes, you may be tempted to think "they all look the same!" (Because they do. But not exactly!) At this stage, content yourself with noticing the basic shapes, and particularly the types of beaks: the thin beaks of thrushes and warblers, compared with the stubby beaks of the seed eaters, like finches and sparrows. Rest assured, it will all become clearer and clearer. And also remember that there is nowhere in Britain where you will be faced with sorting out every species in the book. Also rest assured that it is great fun developing your identification skills (I'll tell you how in the following chapters).

Meanwhile, here's a couple of rules for birdwatching (and indeed for life!): Don't panic! And don't bother with what you don't need to know!

Recommended field guides: Of course, *Bill Oddie's Birds of Britain and Ireland*, published by New Holland, is a definite recommendation of mine!

I have many other recommendations, some of which are listed at the back of the book in Further Reading on page 139. And if you travel further than Europe there are field guides for just about everywhere. (See Broaden Your Horizons, page 120.)

AREN'T BOOKS OLD FASHIONED?

I am yet to see a birder consulting a Kindle out in the field, but I dare say it happens. Certainly I do realize that there must be people reading or looking at this book who are beginning to think "But surely I can do all this on my smart phone?" And you probably can. It would be stubborn and reactionary of me to ignore,resist,or boycott the so-called new technology – well, it's new to me! – even though I did exactly that for more years than I care to admit. More fool me, I now say to myself, but I am catching up, and these days even I am nearly fully digitalized. Already videos and cassettes are pretty much obsolete, but they have been replaced by all manner of DVDs and Apps which of course show you birds with both movement and sound. Nevertheless, I doubt that the manufacturers of such products would claim that they totally replace a good field guide type book. Quite simply, you need one.

You could argue that you also need a mobile phone, if only to keep in touch with friends and family or instantly pass on news of a rare bird sighting (heavens, I remember the time when we had to scour the countryside to find a phone box that hadn't been vandalized.) Nowadays, everyone carries a mobile, which means that they also carry a camera. Perhaps the most radical change to birdwatching in recent years is that nearly everyone is now permanently armed with the means of taking a photograph. The result is that we are at a point where a claim of a rare bird won't even be considered without photographic evidence. Whether it was been taken on a Flip, an Ipod,a smart phone or a not so smart phone, lack of a 'record shot' is simply unacceptable. It doesn't even have to be a good photo. By the time it has been enhanced and magnified on a computer, chances are that its identification will be indisputable. The current adage could well be: "See the bird, grab a snap." It is the photographic equivalent of the Victorian "collectors" motto "What's hit's history, what's missed's mystery." Fortunately pixels are kinder than bullets.

If your phone is REALLY smart it will transport you to an 'App' depicting every British bird, along with audio of their songs and calls thus allowing you instant comparison with whatever you have seen or heard, and even a means of attracting it closer. (It used to be called tape luring) I cant object to any of this except to urge

Right: INSECT EATERS clockwise from left: *Sedge Warbler, Spotted Flycatcher (juvenile), Chiffchaff. Look at their bills.* SEED EATERS clockwise from left: *Lesser Redpoll, Greenfinch, House Sparrow. Compare these birds bills to the insect eaters.*

The basic general rule for bird bills: thin ones for insect eaters, thick ones for seed eaters. Mind you, this doesn't stop the birds varying their diets. For example, nestling seed eaters (such as House Sparrows) are fed on soft insects and grubs; and we all know that Blue and Great Tits – which have fine, insect-eating-type bills – are extremely happy with peanuts.

you not to overdo the recorded playbacks.

I do of course have natural tendancy to play the role of a curmudgeonly luddite (at my age it is part of the job) so please allow me a grumpy mutter about "young birdwatchers having it too easy these days." I am probably jealous. The staggering fact is that nowdays it is no big deal to be able to carry a field guide,a camera, a zoom , a sound recorder and player, and a means of phoning, texting or emailing your mates, all in a device not much bigger than a Mars bar. I would just make one purist plea: please make sure you spend more time looking at the bird than at a screen. Oh, and one more thing, youngsters may have far more equipment, but we had far more birds. (See Conservation, page 126.)

INSECT EATERS

SEED EATERS

ESSENTIAL GEAR

As well as a field guide, you will need a decent pair of binoculars ("bins" for short). Happily, this is another area where things really have got very good indeed. Mind you, there is such a huge range of types, styles, sizes and prices that you may feel rather confused over what to choose. The rule – again (I said I'd be repeating this) – is to buy from a specialist dealer. Don't buy from the local chemist, or even photographic shop. They may well have some good bins but they won't have a huge range, and the price is likely to be higher than at the specialist. These companies are run for and often by birdwatchers. You will find them advertised in the bird magazines (see page 137) or yellow pages. You will be able to get advice, go to the shop and try out different models, and possibly even be able to get a pair on approval so you can field test them. Buying online is risky.

Frankly, there is an awful lot of potential waffle about the various types of optical systems, specifications, dimensions and so on, and it's easy to feel a bit blinded by science. But remember that rule: don't bother with things you don't need to know. To help, I will simply run through the meaning of some of the figures you do need to know about!

Magnification. This is simple enough. All binoculars are clearly marked 7, 8, 10, or whatever the magnification is. This means what it implies: that the subject is magnified seven times or eight times or ten times. The ideal

Right: *Great Spotted Woodpecker using different magnification.* From left to right: *6 x magnification, 9 x magnification and 12 x magnification (all at 6m range); close-up yes, but you'd have trouble holding the binoculars steady.*

magnification for birdwatching is between 7 and 10 (inclusive). There will also be a second number, for example, the bins may be marked 7 x 42 or 8 x 40. This second figure is (I think!) millimetres and refers somehow to lens sizes. You see, I don't really understand it and you don't need to either! (The man in the shop will explain if you want him to but you may remain slightly baffled, as I am.) What you do need to appreciate is that this second figure is to do with how wide and how bright the image is. There is a trade-off here. Generally speaking, the more you magnify, the less wide the picture will be, and it will also be less bright. It is honestly true that a smaller brighter image is often clearer and preferable to a big murky close up. A generally accepted rule is that the second number divided by the first should be at least 3. So 10 x 32 is fine, just. With 8 x 32 the picture will be less magnified, but it will be brighter and wider.

Close focusing is another important factor. Although, obviously, binoculars are mainly for bringing distant objects closer, in fact birds occasionally hop or fly towards you, and it is a pity if you can't keep them in focus without stepping away from them. Close focus is also pretty essential if you want to look at dragonflies and butterflies through binoculars. (And you should. They look fantastic, even if you can't

identify them!) Many bins these days will focus down to two or three metres (6–9 ft).

Depth of focus is also another important element: in practical terms, if binoculars have a small (shallow) depth of focus, you will have constantly to keep turning the focusing wheel. A greater depth means less finger work and a fuller picture.

To be honest, I could ramble on for ages about binoculars (most birdwatchers do!) but I think it would be more useful to simply list a few warnings.

Very small binoculars, like glorified opera glasses. Yes, you can slip them into a pocket, and the more expensive ones may be optically impressive, *but* they will have a small field of view and shallow depth of focus. You may well find it hard to "find", follow and focus on birds in the field, especially birds in flight.

Big magnification: It's definitely not a case of the bigger the better. Anything over 10 may be heavy and hard to hold steady, and may also have a narrow field of view, dull picture and poor close focusing.

These points will become so much clearer if you can go to that specialist and try out lots of kinds. Mind you, standards are so high these days that you may well feel there are several pairs that seem equally impressive. What's more, you may find it hard to really see much difference between a pair that is £250 and one that is £750. So what *is* the difference (apart from 500 quid)? I'm slightly tempted to say "snob value" (and there might be a smidgeon of truth in that). The real difference, however, is reliability and ruggedness. The £750 pair should last a lifetime and be fault free. The cheaper ones may be less waterproof (they may mist up inside if you use them in heavy rain) or the picture may noticeably deteriorate over the years.

Conclusion. By all means buy the best you can afford, but don't be unhappy if they are in the lower price range. There really are some relatively cheap binoculars that are very good. They are certainly the ones to get if you are not yet entirely sure about the

Left: *I am simply amazed that rainguards aren't standard issue with all new binoculars. A simple device that will save you so much irritation.*

Above: *The most important thing when choosing new binoculars is to test them for yourself. Obviously the more you spend the better the quality, although there are some decent budget models available.*

hobby, or if you intend to be a part time, or fair weather birder! Or a serviced and guaranteed second-hand pair could be the bargain you are after. One thing is for certain: I guarantee that you will be amazed and delighted by the view you get through a good pair of binoculars. They will become one of your most treasured possessions.

A FEW OTHER POINTS

The carrying case: use it to protect your binoculars "in transit" if you like, but once you are in the field you simply don't need it. Your bins should be at the ready, round your neck at all times, otherwise you will miss an awful lot of birds. I lost my case years ago!

The neck strap: some bins still come with rather narrow and abrasive straps that will wear a painful groove in your neck in no time. It is definitely worth investing in a wider, softer type. No chafing, and heavy bins really do seem lighter. I have noticed birders in America increasingly supporting their bins on a sort of harness (a bit like for a toddler's "reins!"). To be honest, I'm not a fan, but by all means check 'em out, as they say in the States.

A rainguard: a little leather or plastic cover that is attached to the strap and keeps the rain off the eye pieces. Absolutely essential. If the bins don't come with one, buy one.

SPECTACLE WEARERS

If you wear glasses – as I do – if you look through bins with your glasses on you will get a sort of tunnelling effect, and be immediately aware that you are not seeing the full picture. Some birdwatchers resolve this by pushing their spectacles back onto their heads and using "naked eyes". I tried that, but soon realized that I was missing some birds, and occasionally my specs would fall off if I was leaning back (birds flying overhead were particularly problematic). So I now keep my specs on. Fortunately nowadays just about all binoculars have retractable eyecups which solve the problem of tunnelling. The most basic are fold back rubber (though they tend to fray or go out of shape eventually). The type that click or screw in are best. (By the way, the dealer – or the advert – may refer to something called "eye relief". I have never understood what it means. You don't need to know either!) One more spectacles tip: you will get the widest picture by using the smallest glasses. I have a pair in sturdy "national health John Lennon" type frames which are ideal for birding. It makes sense really I suppose, these small glasses are nearer to glorified contact lenses (which I've tried too, but they literally reduced me to tears. If you can use them, I envy you!).

A word of encouragement. I confess I was pretty depressed when I was first told – or indeed realized – that I needed glasses for long-sighted stuff like birdwatching, but I got used to them very quickly.

There are days when I curse the drizzle, or keep misting up in the frost, but there are others when my glasses protect my eyes from the wind. And one thing's for sure, I certainly see a lot more than I did without them!

On this page are some of the many bits and pieces you'll find at an optical dealers, who'll specialize in both birdwatching and photographic gear. Be aware (and beware) that what is the best support for a camera and telephoto lens will not necessarily be what is best for a telescope. Photographic tripods tend to have quite complicated heads, but keep it simple for a telescope.

Right: What's what?! OK, here's a little challenge for you. It is pretty obvious what some of these items are, whilst there's at least one where even I am not sure what it is! You don't need everything that is shown. Only by trial (and error, possibly) will you find out what is most useful for you.

So what's what? Match the caption to the item. (No, this list isn't in the order shown.)

Binocular rain guard: essential.

Beanbag: for resting long lens camera or 'scope on the shelf of a hide, car roof, or through a window.

Wide binocular strap: probably a lot more comfortable than the one the bins came with.

Car window mount: for camera or telescope.

Telescope hide mount: for camera or telescope. Neater than struggling with a tripod in a hide, but surprisingly heavy.

Tripod: the easiest kind to use with a telescope has only one adjustment lever.

Telescope lens raincap: I think!

All weather telescope case: keeps out the rain and keeps your 'scope warm – better for your fingers!

TELESCOPES

There is a huge range of binoculars, and new improved models appear constantly, and yet basically they haven't changed all that much for years. I have a pair which I got as a Christmas present back in the mid-1950s, and they are still excellent. Telescopes, however, have undergone a revolution. For many years I had to manage with a long cumbersome brass contraption that was basically much the same as Nelson put to his blind eye. Eventually, that evolved into a plastic version. Nowadays, there is a truly bewildering selection of "scopes" – or spotting scopes – in all sorts of shapes, sizes and prices.

A FEW RULES

• A telescope is not a substitute for binoculars.
• You guessed it: go to the specialist dealer.
• Do get one, if your budget will stretch to it.

Some people do have trouble using a scope at first: they get tunnel vision (even without glasses) and they have problems "finding" the birds. But you will get used to it. And believe me, it's worth it. The first time you see a bird through a telescope can be literally breathtaking. A "wow!" moment. A revelation. It's a way to turn on birders, especially kids: look through a scope.

The cautions are similar to those for binoculars. Cheaper telescopes may not be as robust as the pricey models, which should last for ever (we're talking a range from about £200 to £3,000 here!). Also, the smaller ones may have less magnification or field of view than the "howitzer" jobs. But then again, the big ones are heavy and certainly expensive.

Apart from price and size, there are some other basic choices to be made. Straight through or angled (look down) eye piece? Fixed magnification or zoom lens? More than one lens? (They are usually interchangeable). Maybe a wide angled lens, which makes it easier to "find" birds, for example out at sea. The specialist dealer will be only too happy to show you the full range of what is available and talk you through it. Take your time.

PODS

It is virtually impossible to hand hold a telescope for more than a few seconds. You will need a tripod. Yet again there is a big range available, with differing features: quick release click-on heads, extending legs which may either screw or click into place, some with a single control arm to tip and tilt, others with two. Photographic tripods are not the same as telescope tripods (another reason not to go to the photographic dealer for your birding optics). Generally, a cameraman takes rather more time to set up and get steady and needs a more elaborate – but therefore slower – tripod. A birder's priorities are speed and ease of action. Legs down, find the bird. You don't want to be fiddling around with an array of levers, toggles and screws. Unfortunately, the fact is that the heavier a tripod the steadier it will be. The very lightweight ones may seem alluring, but they will wobble in the wind.

Above: *Angled eyepiece: useful for showing birds to other – taller! – people. You don't have to keep adjusting the tripod legs so much.*

Below: *A tripod is useful for obtaining a steady view, although if you are too lazy to carry one, as I often am, resting the scope on a convenient leaning post, such as a fence or a gate will work as a substitute.*

The same goes for monopods and shoulder pods. You can use a scope on either of these, but you won't be able to keep it up for long (to coin a phrase). In any event, believe me, using a scope on a tripod is infinitely preferable and much less painful than lying on your back with it propped on your knees like I had to do with my old brass model.

TWO MORE INVALUABLE BITS OF GEAR

• All-weather case for your scope.
• Carrying sling for the tripod.

When you are out birding, you probably keep your telescope on the tripod. Be honest – it is awkward and heavy. Over the years, I wore a groove in my shoulder by carrying the whole set up like a rifle. Nowadays, I sometimes manage with the carrying strap on my all-weather case, but if you want

Above: A carrying strap for a telescope or tripod is a good idea, especially as it leaves your hands free for using binoculars. The alternative is the 'traditional' transport method of balancing it on your shoulder.

to really lessen the load you should try a specially designed sling (carrying strap). New, supposedly even more cozy and efficient, ones seem to appear each month. I have several. Working out how to fit the sling to the scope and tripod can be a bit of a puzzle. Frankly, there are several possible points of attachment, and each to his or her own. Very tall people manage with the tripod legs at least partially extended (so they are really quick on the draw). Shorter people (like me) have to keep the legs contracted and folded up alongside the scope, so that they don't keep hitting the ground or my knees. It's a matter of trial and – sometimes slightly painful – error. I'll be honest, I have never discovered a way of carrying a scope and

tripod that I could truly call comfortable. But it is (usually) worth it! Mind you – and this will be heresy to some birders – I would recommend asking yourself before setting out for a day's birding: "Do I *really* need my scope?" Of course, the day you don't take it is when you'll see a distant puzzling possible rarity that you could have clinched if only you'd had your scope with you.

As you may have gathered, I have a slight love/hate relationship with telescopes. The truth is I have two: a lightweight one, which I carry on a shoulder pod (for those days I don't really expect to need a scope at all, but think I'd better take one, just in case) and a big 'un on a tripod, with a padded carrying sling.

The specialist dealer is likely to have a case full of ironmongery and contraptions with screws and ratchets, some of which look as if they belong in The Marquis de Sade section at the London Dungeon. Hide clamps, window clamps, I've bought 'em all, and I've rarely used any of them. For cameras, yes perhaps, but for telescopes I'm not at all sure. I suppose I'd suggest you wait and see if you feel the need for them, and, if you can afford them, by all means try them. Actually, that brings me to my final conclusion on telescopes. If you can't afford one, don't worry – in many cases, if there are other birders around, they will let you have a squint through theirs! – but if you do decide to stretch the budget, you won't regret it.

Above: *With practice you can find a bird using a scope in the blink of an eye.*

Below: *How many thousand pounds worth of optical equipment, all to look at one little bird?*

OUTDOOR CLOTHING

Coats and jackets: Aha, the dreaded anorak! Many bird books and articles (I confess, including some of mine) adopt a rather patronising tone about "wearing something dull and rustle-free so that it doesn't scare the birds". Own up, only a bit of a twit would march out to go birding in a fluorescent orange kaghoul (not that I haven't seen it happen). Suffice it to say that you may well be out in inclement conditions and you should dress accordingly. Ironically and perversely, the best birding is often caused by bad weather: storms, rainshowers, strong winds, fog, all sometimes ground migrant birds or blow them off course. You may find yourself miles from shelter, or even out on an open boat. Unfortunately, yachting and skiing-type gear does tend to come in lurid colours and noisy material – bird scaring costumes indeed. Hence the growth of specialist companies manufacturing clothing for outdoor pursuits – meaning nature study in general and birding in particular.

Probably birders take as much time and trouble over, and as many words have been written about, waterproof jackets as about binoculars and field guides. I'll keep it brief! The problem is that it is not so easy to road (or field) test waterproofs as optics. Maybe the shops should have showers you could dive under, or fridges you could leap into. Failing that, at least you should make sure you ask the right questions, and watch out for evasive or ambiguous answers!

Is it really waterproof? A jacket may well be marked: "windproof", "shower proof", "weather proof", etc. Most of these are euphemisms for "let's be honest, it leaks". In my experience, some of the ones that say "waterproof" also leak. The danger points are shoulders, seams and particularly pockets. In fact, I have been astonished and disappointed how many coats I've had that – despite having apparently weathered a downpour – have still left me with damp

Left: *Winter plumage. Woolly hat, which doesn't cover my ears – so that I can still hear the birds – my faithful waterproof jacket, and a small backpack containing light waterproof trousers, small telescope, and, very importantly, lunch.*

pockets, and a consequently soggy note-book and mouldy Mars bar. So grill that dealer. Make them swear their coat is totally waterproof, and take it back if it isn't.

Talking of pockets, the other requirement of good birding garments is that they have plenty of pockets. Enough to carry small books, wallet, keys, gloves, maps, emergency rations, etc, etc. Remember also that you will be wearing binoculars round your neck, so beware of voluminous collars that get in the way.

Chances are you will end up with a coat (call it an anorak if you like, but the dealer probably won't!) in some kind of guaranteed waterproof and yet breathable material (possibly lined with something ending in "ex").

You may consider getting **waterproof trousers** in the same material. Personally, I find these a bit too hot on my legs, and I tend to carry a pair of lightweight slip overs instead. In fact, especially in cold weather, most birders would agree that the "layers" principle gives you the most options. You can always take things off and tie them round your waist or stuff 'em in a bag.

Boots: again, check the waterproofing claims (you are likely to splash through somewhere soggy eventually). In my experience, the "ex" linings work well at first, but do get less ef-ficient after a while. Wellies are fine, but can be chilly on cold days or stuffy on hot ones, and you'll get foot sore if you walk too far in them. In summer in recent years I have taken to bare feet and open sandals, and learnt to enjoy the dew between my toes!

Top: *Essential supplies: food, books, various contraptions: you can never have too many pockets.*

Above: *Footwear. Thank heavens for soft, lightweight boots. For years I crippled myself by wearing heavy-duty clodhoppers or wellies.*

Hats: by all means, but don't forget that earflaps or hoods will block out the bird song and you'll miss things that way. If you wear glasses, you'll find a peak invaluable for keeping the rain off. I have an inexhaustible supply of baseball caps!

Gloves: if it's not too chilly, I prefer the fingerless type, or my "convertibles", which have a Velchro'd mitten attachment. Be honest, they've thought of most things.

And in drier weather … if it's dry but chilly, I admit I am pretty much addicted to my fleece. It's got several pockets, and in fact it's waterproof enough to easily withstand anything but a real deluge. In summer, my favourite "specialist" garment is a light waistcoat with masses of pockets (like photographers often wear) but with a collar, which prevents neck chafing from binocular straps. If it's too hot even for my waistcoat – shorts weather – it's a shirt with a breast pocket for my note-book, and a "bumbag" for the other bits and pieces.

Choosing the ideal outdoor clothing may involve hours – nay years – of fun and frustration, but you will eventually sort out what you feel comfortable in. Ultimately, it's a personal thing and – be honest – it would be pretty boring – in fact, positively creepy! – if we all wore the same gear. In any case, let's face it, in the long run whatever you are wearing isn't likely to really affect what you see!

Right: *A woolly hat is essential in cold weather, and if it is one advertising the BTO then so much the better.*

Opposite above:
*Swallows on the
wire. These birds are
preparing to fly south for
winter. Generally, birds
are pretty much oblivious
to the weather. But you're
not, and neither am I, so
it's best to be prepared.*

This page: *Fieldfares are
winter visitors and used
to the snow and winter
winds of Europe.*

THE BASICS OF IDENTIFICATION

The basics of identification!? Mm, sounds like a bit of a scary chapter, eh? Pages and pages – whole books indeed – have been written about this (I've done it myself) but I am not going to go on about it here for a couple of reasons. First of all, I really do think it is one of those topics that sound more complex – and therefore off-putting – the more you analyze it. And secondly, I think a lot of the points are better and more appropriately covered by a good field guide. Thirdly – and perhaps above all – it is a lot more fun to find out for yourself, by trial and error as it were. Added to which – that's fourthly! – I honestly believe that it is only when you work out identification in the field that it really sticks.

If I may digress for a moment … A few years ago I decided to try to get into wild flowers. I started by looking at them in the field (a nice change from birding actually) and then I would go home and look them up in the book. More often than not, I

Red Kite. One of those birds with a unique feature: no other British bird of prey has a deeply forked tail.

probably got them right. Nevertheless, the next time I went out, I would see what were no doubt the same flowers, but I wouldn't recognize them all, and I certainly couldn't remember all their names. Then, one mid-summer day, I was being shown round a nature reserve at Hauxley in Northumberland. In fact, there weren't many birds around, which suited the warden because he was largely a botanist. "OK then," I said, "show me the flowers." This he duly did, pointing out some of the different families, leaf and petal shapes, and so on, and even adding some anecdotes about how they got their English names. The next day, I went exploring further along the coast on my own. I discovered that I not only remembered the names of the flowers that the warden had shown me, I also seemed to have developed a much better eye for finding new ones for myself.

I also discovered that I could find them in the book more easily. What's more – although I certainly wouldn't call myself a botanist – I have been noticing, naming, and enjoying wild flowers ever since.

I tell that story to make two points. Firstly, I reckon it helps enormously to be initially shown things by experts, but secondly, you may well then develop your skills better on your own.

GO IT ALONE? OR NOT?

So, let's take that first point. Should you at least start birding in a group? When I was a youngster there weren't all that many opportunities. Nevertheless, at my local reservoir I met and spent some time with a local expert, and it certainly helped – as well as being socially more enjoyable. Nowadays, there are plenty of opportunities: outings and field trips with Bird Clubs, RSPB groups, or County Wildlife Trusts, and "open days" at nature reserves, with guided walks and so on. In fact, on any visit to an official reserve – particularly the large RSPB showcase reserves – you will meet other birders, at least some of whom will be happy to share – indeed show off – their knowledge (see page 98). You may meet people who become birding companions, or indeed you may already know someone at a similar early stage of curiosity, and it is undoubtedly more enjoyable to learn together.

The only disadvantage of large groups is that, frankly, it is not the most discreet way to watch birds. My own personal

Right: Wren.
A tiny bird with an incredibly loud song. Most people will have heard a Wren's song, even if they didn't realize what it was.

nightmare occurred at a Bird Fair where the organizers had advertised "3.00 p.m. Guided Walk led by Bill Oddie", and I arrived to find over a hundred people waiting for me. I duly led them off round the nearby gravel pits, but the ones at the back couldn't keep within earshot, let alone see what we at the front were seeing. And vice versa. I moved to the middle and started shouting, but that didn't help, as it frightened off most of the birds – as well as several small children. So, let's say I'm a fan of small groups. My personal preference is for one or two companions, or to be on my own. (See page 138 for more on groups.) Which brings me to that second point: working it out for yourself. Yes, it is easier with others, but at some point you really ought go it alone and really test yourself. It is ultimately more satisfying and – like I said – I think that's when it really sticks.

UNFAMILIAR BIRDS

Which brings me back to this business of identification (ID for short). Let's assume you are looking at an unfamiliar bird. If you are with a group, chances are someone will identify it for you (and you may or may not remember and recognize it the next time you see the same species). But what if you are on your own? Many – perhaps most – books about identification will suggest that you take notes, make drawings, try to ascribe the bird to a family, study the topography charts in the field guide, etc. But let's face it, at an early stage, you don't do any of that.

I know this from my experience with flowers, butterflies and dragonflies. I see the flower or the insect. I try to remember what it looks like – get a mental picture in my head. Then I flick through the pages of the field guides until I find an illustration that looks like what I saw. Then – and only then – I may read the text, which warns me that what I think I've seen is very rare, or only occurs in Scotland (I'm in London), or only appears in August (it's May). So I have to look through the pictures again. It's then that I realize that there are three or four species that look very similar. But maybe only one of them occurs in the south

of England in spring. So that must be what I saw. Or maybe there are two possibilities, two species so similar that I really need to go back and try again, and this time make a special effort to look at diagnostic details, maybe the shape of the spotty markings at the back end, the colour of the wingtips, the shape of the petals. With any luck, I see it again, I remember it better, and I manage to match up what I saw with a picture in the book. Or maybe I don't. Maybe I still haven't seen enough.

The point I am making is that the identification process – nine times out of ten – is based on seeing something

Left: Jays can be a bit of a puzzler, depending upon which bit you notice. "It had a crest." "It had blue wings." " It had a white rump." All Jays!

– whether it is a flower, an insect or a bird – looking it up in the book and recognizing the picture. This of course puts a huge onus on the field guide artists to get it right! Fortunately, these days most of them are brilliant, showing not only accurate plumages but also capturing the shape, stance and character of a bird (what birdwatchers call the "jizz"). So – and I'm flying somewhat in the face of the accepted "notes and sketches" method here – I am going to accept what I believe is the truth: that most IDs are done by eye, rather than by deduction.

LEARNING TO LOOK

So, the first vital step towards a skill in identifying birds is to train yourself to really see. Look at a bird. Take it in. Don't go rummaging through the book immediately (you may look up, and the bird will have flown away). Look, and ask yourself questions. What does this bird really look like? How big is it? Compare it

Right: *Magpie. Surely one of the birds that really can't be mistaken for anything else?*

with something you know. Is it the size of a House Sparrow, a Starling, a Blackbird or a goose? What shape is it? Again make comparisons. What colour or colours are there? Where are the most obvious markings? All this will help you retain a full mental picture. Then ask yourself some more questions. What kind of place is it in? Hopping on a lawn? Perching on a branch? Splashing in a pond? If it was flying was it flapping or soaring? What time of year was it? What part of the country, and what type of countryside? (I'll tell you why all this could be relevant in a moment.) I am not suggesting that you methodically go through a conscious checklist of such questions, but just train yourself to look and think this way. It will all help make that bird stick in your mind. Let's face it, probably the most useful attribute a potential birdwatcher could have would be a photographic memory. Or let's call it accurate visual recall. All you have to do is match the picture in your mind's eye with the one in the book.

As it happens, I truly believe that most identifications are indeed done this way – purely visually – and that – and be encouraged by this – an awful lot of them are right! Try this: work through the pages of your field guide, and mentally tick off the birds you know. Add to those the ones that are surely unmistakable. By the time you get to the end I'm willing to bet that those 200 and odd species won't seem quite so intimidating.

IT'S NOT IN THE BOOK

The problems and puzzles arise, of course, when you see a bird that you simply can't find in the book. There could be plenty of reasons for this. Most commonly it's probably because you just didn't see it quite as well as perhaps you thought, or that your recall isn't quite accurate enough. The first – harsh – lesson of birding is: there will be birds that "get away". The consolation is that it is more than likely that you will see the species again, probably better, and next time you will be able to identify it. You may well find yourself thinking back and muttering "Ah, so that's what that was!"

There are several points to bear in mind if you see a puzzling bird. Firstly – overwhelmingly – the chances are that the bird you saw is in the book, even if you can't immediately find it. I have known many examples of this. People have come up to me and said "I've seen this funny bird. It's not in the book." But it was. Maybe not in quite the pose, or position, or plumage that

they saw it, but it was there. And talking of plumage, the next vital thing to appreciate is that many species occur in a variety of plumages. Some don't – so that's a relief. Magpies, Jays, Herons, many of the geese, all basically look much the same, whatever their age or sex or time of the year (apart from the really tiny babies). Generally, when a species does have different plumages it will be the adult males that are most

colourful and/or easiest to recognize. As a rule, the female will be a dowdier version of the male. She may even show some of the same markings, but much more subdued. But male and female will still be the same size and shape and share the same habits and habitat.

The most confusing and challenging birds to identify are the species that have lots of different plumages according to sex (male, female), age (adult and juveniles), and time of the year (summer and winter).

Opposite: *Blackbird. Well, at least the name helps ... so long as it's an adult male. Females are brown, and the young birds can look almost orangey and quite speckled.*

Right: *Chaffinch. A classic case of brightly coloured male, dowdy brown female. A rule that applies to an awful lot of birds. Unfortunately, they are not always in pairs like this.*

It would be pretty meaningless – and arguably irritating – for me to go through lots of examples here.

QUESTIONS TO ASK YOURSELF

A rummage through the field guide will show you what I mean. But what I will do is give you a list a questions to ask yourself if you can't find a bird in the book.

Let's assume that you are at least looking at the right type (family) of birds. So … was it a female? Was it a juvenile? Was it in winter plumage (often much dowdier than summer or breeding plumage).Was it in moult? (When some birds can look oddly sort of half and half.) If you still can't find it, you have to ask yourself: are you looking in the right family? This kind of confusion can occur because birds don't always stick

Below: *Herring Gull in three different plumages. Adult at the back, juvenile at the front, and 'in between' (second year) in the middle, in sort of 'half and half' plumage.A beginner could be forgiven for thinking that these were three different species.*

Below: *Black-tailed Godwit (top) and Dunlin (bottom). Many of the waders are striking examples of birds that look dazzling in breeding plumage, but are just grey-and-white in winter.*

to the "right" habitat or do what you expect them to do. I can best illustrate this by an example. A bloke stopped me on Hampstead Heath and said: "I've seen this biege-coloured bird, with a scarlet head, on my lawn this morning. I can't find it in the book." "Could be a Green Woodpecker," I told him. "No, it wasn't up a tree, it was on my lawn," he replied. "Yep, that's exactly where I'd expect it. Green Woodpeckers often feed on the ground, collecting ants with their long sticky tongues. Green Woodpeckers aren't always on wood." But they *are* in the book! It was just that that bloke hadn't even looked in the woodpecker section.

In fact, what a bird is doing and in what habitat and at what time of the year will often be the vital clues to identifying it. Another example: Different bloke but same place. "Could I have seen a Wheatear on Hampstead Heath?" "Yes, you could. When was it?" "A couple of weeks ago." "Late April. Yep, good time. They are spring migrants, and we usually get one or two passing through. Was it a male or a female?" "Oh I don't know. It was sort of pinky underneath, bluey grey on the back." "Sounds like a male." "It had a black mask." "Definitely a male. Nice one. Where exactly was it?" "In the woods." "Really?" "Yes." "What was it doing?" "Running up a tree trunk." "Ah! It was Nuthatch!" "But I looked it up in the book," the bloke protested. "Grey back, black mask, pink below. Wheatear." "Yes, but so is a Nuthatch. And Nuthatches creep up trees like little woodpeckers, but

Wheatears don't. They run around on short grass. When they occur on the Heath I see them on the playing fields or maybe on top of Parliament Hill. They *can* perch on top of trees, but out in the open, and they soon drop down again. Honestly, that was a Nuthatch." I think the bloke was quite happy, because whatever it was it was a new bird for him!

THE PHANTOM NIGHTINGALE

As in that case, what the bird is doing and where may be vital information. In other cases it will be the date and season that are the crucial clues. Another example, and this is, in fact, probably the commonest mistake I come across. Last March an elderly neighbour of mine popped a note through my door. "Mr Oddie, I thought you might like to know I have a Nightingale singing in my garden."

Opposite Left: *Green Woodpecker.*
Of course they do peck wood, but
you are far more likely see one on
the ground, or flying away from you,
when its bright yellow rump will be
the most obvious feature.

Above: *Pinkish underneath, bluish*
back, black mask. Male Wheatear. It
also has a bright white rump, but it
doesn't climb up tree trunks. Oh, it's
also a summer visitor only.

Right: *Also pinkish underneath, bluish*
back, black mask. Nuthatch. Same
description, but a very different bird.
Or so I thought until that bloke got
them mixed up. It does climb tree
trunks, and it's an all-year resident.

I didn't have the heart to write back, "No, you haven't!", so I just didn't reply. A few days later I got a phone call: "Mr Oddie, the Nightingale is still singing." "Er, have you seen it?" I asked. "No … but I hear it every night lately". I still didn't want to disillusion her, so I let it pass. Until two days later. I was at my desk gazing out of the window in a bit of a daydream, when I noticed my neighbour was at her window on the other side of the street. She pointed at the nearby roof, beamed happily and mouthed, "Nightingale". I smiled back and nodded, resisting the urge to mouth back. "It's a Blackbird. It's not a Nightingale." What's more, I had known that for weeks, even before I saw or heard it myself.

The reasons:
1. Nightingales are almost unheard of (or from) in central London (despite the rumour of one in Berkeley Square).
2. Where Nightingales do occur in Britain, they are very rarely seen perching on rooftops. They are addicted to scrubby heathy type woodland.
But most conclusively
3. They are summer visitors, that don't arrive until mid-April.

The fact is, a night singer in suburbia in March will be a Blackbird, Song Thrush or most likely a Robin, which – just to make it more confusing – if seen from the back, is small and brown, and can look not unlike a Nightingale. Mind you, if it turns round, the red breast is a bit of a giveaway!

Anyway, back to my point and the business of looking it up in the book. Vital information to be noted down, as well as getting as good a view of the bird as possible, are those other questions I suggested you ask yourself (see page 39): Where was it? What was it doing? And what time of the year was it? When you get round to consulting the field guide, these may well be the final pieces of the jigsaw.

To sum up, I guess my quick and realistic guide to ID is to look at the bird for as long as you can, and form a mental picture. Do a sketch or take a description if you like (more of that on page 52), but you probably won't! Try to find it in the book. When you think you have found it, read the text, and as a little fail-safe double check that the bird "should" occur where and when you saw it.

Left: *Another general rule amongst songbirds: the duller the bird, the better the song. So don't worry if you don't see the Nightingale: it's hardly worth it. (Actually, it's quite exciting when you do.)*

You really will be encouraged by how many birds you can sort out. Of course there will always be puzzles. ID is a process of elimination. When all else fails, go through and say what it isn't!

MYSTERY BIRDS

If you *still* can't find the mystery bird in the book, there are other possibilities to consider. It could of course be a genuine rarity. In fact, this is probably the *last* thing to consider. It may seem a truism, but never forget that rarities are rare. Many experienced birders go through life without ever finding a genuine rarity for themselves. You should be so lucky as to find one (but you might be!) But first, consider other possibilities such as: is it an "aberrant", the scientific word for an unusual plumage, such as an albino (white Blackbirds and pied crows are surprisingly common), or a leucistic form (washed out biscuit colour). Or is it an escape? There are lots of birds in collections, cages and zoos, and they do get out and get misidentified, or at least puzzle birders and public alike. These

Below: *Robin singing at night. We assume that they are inspired – fooled, more like – by street lamps or a very bright moon. I have a local bird that never seems to stop singing: does it ever sleep? Surely it must drop off sometime? Off the branch, with exhaustion, probably.*

can be anything from exotic finches to weird waterfowl. Or is it a hybrid? Ducks and geese of different species are prone to getting together and producing offspring that look either like a cross between two species or something completely different.

But hang on … what was that other life and birding rule? Don't panic! There really aren't all these weird-looking birds out there to confuse you. Never forget that the vast majority of birds are not that difficult to identify. And they *are* in the book! And the more you birdwatch, the easier you will find it to sort them out, and the fewer there will be that you can't. And it's ever such fun, anyway!

Left: *Rose-ringed (Ring-necked) Parakeet. Originally 'escapes', this species has become an honorary British Citizen in southeast England. A good example of another general rule: pretty birds often make horrible noises.*

Above: *Red-breasted Goose and Snow Goose. Both species occur as genuine wild rarities, but the vast majority have escaped from wildfowl collections. They are still worth looking at, though.*

Above: *The perfect contradiction in terms: a white Blackbird. Partial albinos (those with a few white feathers) of several species are surprisingly common.*

Right: *Yellow-billed Cuckoo. A genuine rarity. I was once lucky enough to find one in late September in Dorset. It should have been in North America (where it breeds) or South America (where it winters). It may well have hitched a lift on a transatlantic liner, but it was certainly a wild bird.*

NOTES AND LISTS

Just about every "how to watch birds" book (including some of my own) will suggest you carry a little note-book. In it, you are exhorted to record your observations in the field. Note the date, the place, the weather, the wind direction, list all the birds you see, and in particular take notes on birds you can't identify, and do drawings – field sketches – of them, noting the markings and areas of colour. Ideally, you will begin to use the topography maps and mark in the feather areas with their proper scientific names: "yellow wingbar on greater coverts, white supercilium" and so on.

Well, all this is fine. But you don't have to do it! It does sometimes bother me that this kind of detailed instruction can put off potential birdwatchers. At the very least, I've heard people plead "but I can't draw". It doesn't matter. It is perfectly possible to watch, enjoy and even identify birds without taking or keeping notes.

Having said that, note-books can be very useful and satisfying. I have two kinds: my field note-books, and my "big" note-books. The former is a little "policeman's note-book", with an attached pencil. And yes, I do jot down dates, weather, numbers of birds I see and – if necessary – the odd description and field sketch. And, if I'm lucky enough to see a bird I don't recognize, my notes and drawings may well help me to identify it. It has been said that the worst drawing is worth a page full of words, and there is some truth in that. I have a birder friend who is certainly no artist. As he put it: "I do thumbnail sketches." And as I commented: "Well they look more like thumbnails than birds!" But

they have helped him sort out quite a few rarities over the years.

Sketching and note-taking are good and useful habits to get into, but in recent years I have increasingly noticed that by no means all birders do it. And that is fine. Nevertheless, I would recommend note-taking but, as it happens, not so much as an aid to identification, but as a sort of diary from which you may well get a lot of pleasure. After all my birding trips – be they a morning on Hampstead Heath or a week abroad – I write up my big note-book. Over the years, I have added sketches, paintings, photos, graphs, and indeed the odd anecdote that had very little to do with birds at all. I have books going back 40 odd years to when I started birding as a kid. They are amongst my most treasured possessions, one of the first things I would rescue if the house caught fire! And it is not just because I plunder them for books and articles. I love browsing back, remembering, reminiscing, and comparing facts and figures over the

Above: *Making field notes. Personally, I use a 'policeman's notebook', with a little pencil attached. I always have it in my pocket, and find it equally useful for jotting down shopping lists and reminders.*

years. Exactly what form your bird diary takes is, of course, entirely up to you, but I really do recommend that you keep one.

LISTS

Another thing I would recommend keeping is a few lists. Nearly all birders do. Probably your most cherished is your UK life list (all the species you have seen in Britain, ever). You may have also a world list (everywhere, ever) or various holiday or trip lists. Listing can become something of an obsession but, in any event, I do believe that list-keeping helps focus your birdwatching. You become aware of what you have learned to identify, what you've seen, and what you haven't. And it gives you incentives:

what you'd like to see! To my mind, the potentially most satisfying and personal list is your local patch list.

Keeping a local list also allows you to experience a little of the thrill of rarity finding. I guarantee that every new bird you add will give you a bit of a frisson (that's a nice feeling!). What's more, there may be birds that are common elsewhere but not on your patch. For example, as a teenager, week after week, I used to visit a rather desolate concrete reservoir just outside Birmingham. I will never forget my joy one Sunday morning when I found a single Coot there. Coots are, of course, common enough on most park ponds, but, for some strange reason, they were not attracted to my reservoir (can't

Aug. 25   Local Gravel pits

pale almost white V on back

black bill shorter than Dunlins and straight not curved

back and wings rufous with dark marks

black legs

Feeding with Dunlins and noticeably smaller

Local Gravel pits, muddy corner

Wind East, quite strong

Sunny after showers

No call heard   Also present 100 Lapwings 2 Redshanks Lots of moulting Mallards

blame 'em really: it was very bleak). In fact, this was not only the first Coot that I'd seen there, but it also turned out to be the first one recorded there for ten years. A rarity indeed.

KEEPING NOTES

These drawings aren't exactly works of art, but if you're thinking "they're a lot better than I could do!" then don't be intimidated. They probably started out as scribbles – field sketches – done whilst watching the actual birds and the observer has then worked on them a bit before this final version went into their big notebook. In fact, he or she has noted quite enough to make positive identifications.

In both cases he or she has made a comparison with a familiar species: Dunlin and Chaffinch. If you look those up in a field guide there's a good chance that the two mystery birds will be close by, possibly even on the same or an adjacent page.

The wader is in fact a Little Stint. This is one of only two regular British waders

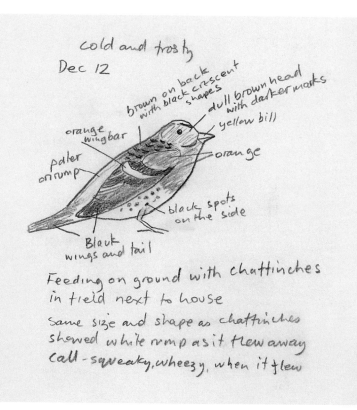

cold and frosty
Dec 12

brown on back
with black crescent
shapes

dull brown head
with darker marks

yellow bill

orange
wingbar

paler
on rump

orange

black spots
on the side

Black
wings and tail

Feeding on ground with chaffinches
in field next to house
Same size and shape as chaffinches
showed white rump as it flew away
call - squeaky, wheezy, when it flew

of a similar shape, but smaller than a Dunlin and one of them (Temmink's Stint) is pretty rare. There's a good rule: always start by assuming it's the common one! The clincher here is the white 'braces' – diagnostic of Little Stint.

The finch is a Brambling (lovely name). It is sometimes referred to as the 'winter Chaffinch' and it probably will be next to it in the field guide. The white rump is a key feature, as is the wheezy call.

In both cases the date adds useful circumstantial evidence. Autumn is the time when most Little Stints pass through Britain (they don't breed here). It would be much rarer to see it in spring or winter. Conversely, a Brambling in anything but wintry months would be far less likely (they don't breed in Britain either, except very rarely in the far north).

It is also a good idea to note the weather and especially the wind direction. The east wind often brings good birds. It'd be worth nipping back to the gravel pits tomorrow to see if any more waders have arrived!

BIRD BEHAVIOUR

It is sometimes said – rather snobbishly perhaps – that "birders" are into ID and listing, whilst "ornithologists" study behaviour. It is true that some heavy birders – those hard-core twitchers certainly – do rarely get past identification as their main interest and concern (and believe me, it is a very elaborate study), whilst – ironically – people who may not consider themselves birders (let alone ornithologists) but simply enjoy feeding birds in the garden actually notice and may even know more about behaviour.

I'm certainly not saying that studying behaviour is a more noble pursuit, but it is endlessly absorbing. It is certainly something that will add immeasurably to your enjoyment of your local patch, and it is also on your local patch that you are most likely to notice behaviour.

ROBINS – FOR EXAMPLE

Just as an example, take some of the aspects of the lifestyle of a Robin (which is hardly an identification challenge!)

In winter, you may simply see a single bird, and hear it singing occasionally. Notice how the song is rather wistful.

Below: *Black Grouse lekking in Scotland. A spectacular communal display: males showing off to the usually not-very-impressed females. Even if you don't live in Scotland, you won't have to go far to see some pretty intriguing action.*

Then, as spring approaches, so too may other Robins. Some may be rival males. Robins are highly territorial and will defend their patch vehemently. Fights may occur. You may feel that you want to rush out and break them up. They are unlikely to be fatal encounters, but I guarantee you will be fascinated watching them. Now, the male's song becomes richer and more seductive to attract a mate. The pairs will form and there will be display, both birds sometimes bowing and wing trembling. You may be lucky enough to see them mate. Next comes choosing a nest site. Robins are almost legendary for nesting in bizarre places. You may well have provided custom-built nest boxes, but they are just as likely to choose a discarded kettle, or the window sill of an outside toilet. Then there is the period of incubation – do both male and female take turns on the eggs? Or does the male have his work cut out fending off potential egg thieves such as squirrels, Magpies and Jays? Sometimes there are tragedies: eggs are stolen or destroyed, or maybe one of the parents is killed by next door's – or even your own – cat. Or there is unseasonably cold weather, and the eggs chill and addle.

All being well, they do hatch and you are treated to the frenzy of parents bringing food back to youngsters. Some – rarely all – will fledge and leave the nest. This is the only – brief – time that fully grown Robins don't have red breasts. They are speckled, rather like tiny thrushes. You may see them cowering deep in the shade, hiding from predators, still being fed by the parents. Soon the red breasts will develop and the youngsters gain the confidence and agility to fend for themselves. By this stage, the adults are looking a right old mess, feathers broken and worn from the rigours of raising a family. They often disappear for a while in mid-summer. In fact, they are probably lying low while they moult their feathers, reappearing in early autumn looking spruce and neat

Right: *In the case of most species, it's only the males that get carried away displaying, but both male and female Robins often face each other, bowing and trembling their wings. Fledgling Robins do a similar movement when they are 'begging' for their parents to feed them, so maybe this is the amorous adults' version of romantic 'baby talk'? (Scientists tell us that the titbits given by the male to the female allow her to assess how good he will be at finding food for their nestlings, help to reinforce the bond between the two birds, and provide the extra food needed by her to make the eggs.)*

Right: *Robin nesting. Actually, this one is a bit unadventurous, by Robin standards, as they are brilliantly inventive at finding quirky nest sites.*

Left: *Fighting Robins. Ironically, what we think of as one of our sweetest and most charming birds is also one of the most belligerent, though they rarely do each other serious injury.*

again. They will probably stick around, but it is possible that, in later autumn, more Robins may appear in your garden. They could be wandering neighbours, or they could literally be foreigners. Some years there is a huge influx of continental Robins from Europe and you can actually see the difference: they tend to be greyer, with paler orange breasts and also shier than the bold Brits. They have usually moved on by early winter leaving "your" original bird, still patrolling his territory and singing wistfully, sometimes even by street lamplight on milder evenings (let's face it, that Nightingale in Berkeley Square was most likely a Robin).

OK, that was just a brief resume of a Robin's year, all observable from your kitchen window. I recount it only to illustrate how much is going on out there. Different species have different lifestyles, and they are all fascinating. The complexity and allure of bird behaviour is testified to by the number of books there are devoted to a single species or family. It is an inexhaustible study, and you can get involved in and absorbed by it without even leaving your own garden, let alone your local patch.

Below: Robin feeding its young. This is the time when young birds are most in danger, as they may barely be able to fly. Fortunately, they are well camouflaged and pretty good at hiding. The red breast feathers will soon begin to 'sprout' amongst the speckles.

MORE THAN JUST NAMES

I suppose what I'm driving at is that identification really is only a part of the fascination and appeal of birds and birding. Behaviour is another aspect. But it is rewarding not simply as a "scientific" study, but because it is dramatic and intriguing.

When I did *Bird in the Nest* some years ago for the BBC (in which we showed the daily goings on inside the nests of various familiar birds) someone christened it "an avian soap opera". Indeed it attracted soap opera viewing figures (up to eight million people tuned in to watch). Its attraction was clearly well beyond just birdwatchers. So what was the appeal? Well, I am pretty sure it was "behaviour", as well as an involvement with birds as individuals. The nation collectively wept when our baby Kingfishers died.

I must admit that *Bird in the Nest* brought home to me the undeniable fact that people really do get involved with what they often think of as 'their' birds.

I'm sure many of you – as I do – talk of "our Robins" or "our Blackbirds", that comfortingly establish themselves each spring, setting up their homes next to ours, in the garden or backyard. Alas, to be honest, small birds rarely live for more than a few years, so it is unlikely to be the same individuals that return for more than, say, two or three seasons. On the other hand, though the birds may change, the attractiveness of the nest sites probably doesn't, which is why – with any luck – they will be used year after year by different generations. To our eyes, the birds look identical, which is why we human beings come to think of them as 'our birds', friends almost. We literally become involved in their lives. Now, I have heard 'heavy' birders, or serious ornithologists, dismissing this attitude as soppy and sentimental. Well, all I can say to that is that I am one of the soppiest. What's more, observing and getting involved with the daily lives of birds may be sentimental, but it is surely also the very essence of studying bird behaviour. The science of ... yes, ornithology. You may be more of a scientist than you realized.

I also think that a large part of the appeal of watching birds and their behaviour is purely aesthetic. I don't just mean that birds are beautiful, or charming or cute or impressive – though different species are all

Left: *Kingfisher. Undeniably beautiful. Whether sitting still on a branch, watching and waiting, or plunging into the water in search of a fish, they are fascinating to watch.*

Above: *Very young Great Tits with no feathers yet and eyes barely open.*

these things – I mean that sometimes there are moments of incredible visual action or amazing shapes. Many photographers strive to capture such moments. It may be birds displaying, fighting, preening and contorting, flying or flocking. The picture will be affected by the angle, the view, the weather, the lighting conditions – all the things that add up to an unforgettable image. Photographers try to freeze the moment. You – as a birder – should search out such images and try to preserve them in your mind's eye. They are the unerasable memories that will stick with you for ever. I realize that I am waxing a bit lyrical, but it's true, and I really believe that the crucial step towards noticing these things is awareness of what can happen: training your eye to look for it.

Above: *Blue Tits already almost fully feathered, being fed by mother.*

Above: *Moorhens are one of the most distinctive and easy to see waterbirds in Europe. Their bulky body and short wings mean that flight is difficult.*

Left: *Adult Moorhens are good parents, taking great care of the young.*

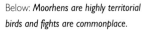

Below: *Moorhens are highly territorial birds and fights are commonplace.*

Above: *Large flocks of Woodpigeons are a common sight as they leave trees or fields.*

Below: *Woodpigeons feeding in a field of cut corn. Scarecrows and other deterrents won't keep them away.*

SONGS AND CALLS

This is possibly the area that intimidates beginners more than any other. I won't exactly alleviate any concern by stating that I reckon well over 50 per cent of the birds that I see, I actually first locate or mainly identify by the noises they make. So, yup, I can't deny it, it is ever so useful to get to know bird song and bird calls. With no due modesty at all, I'd claim to be pretty good at it. Whenever I do radio interviews it seems the host tries to catch me out (show me up?) by playing to me bird CDs and challenging me to identify them. So far I've managed to get them all. As it happens, none of them have been that difficult, but nevertheless the interviewer has been appropriately and satisfyingly impressed. So how is it done? My only answer is: "experience". And frankly, that is the secret, i.e. there really is no secret. So no short cuts here.

How do you acquire this skill? OK, the first step: when you are out – listen! Any bird noise you don't recognize, try to see what is making it. Connect the sound to the sight. Next time, hopefully, you will recognize it. If not, try again. Keep doing

Below: *Sky Lark and its sonogram. Justly famous for its 'never ending' song, which you can often hear even though the bird is so high in the sky that it is invisible to the naked eye.*

Above: *One way of learning songs is to record them or buy a ready-made bird sounds package. Playing them back may attract the species in question, but don't overdo it as the poor bird may get a bit frantic, and indeed frustrated, when it cannot see its non-existent rival.*

Left: *Blackburnian Warbler. American 'warblers' are generally much more colourful – garish almost! – than their British counterparts. They do, however, conform to that general rule that gaudy birds have unimpressive songs. Most of them don't so much warble as wheeze.*

Below: *Northern Parula. Another flashy little 'Yank', with a modest little trill of a song. By the way, both these species have – very rarely – occurred in Britain.*

it. It'll come. Eventually. Honest. But don't worry if it is a slow process, and rest assured that even the most efficient aural expert will hear something now and again that he or she can't place. Young birds in particular make all sorts of squeaks and tsips that are all but impossible to identify.

One of the problems is that no matter how hard the books try to describe or write down bird calls phonetically, it very rarely conjures up anything that really helps. What exactly does a "melodious trill" or a "descending cascade" sound like? Have a look at the transcriptions in some field guides and say them out loud and they either sound like total gibberish – "geryunkangang" – or identical – at least six species go "tik" or "tak". In fact, when you actually hear them, each tik or tak has an identifiable quality, but you just can't convey it on paper. You can of course convey it on CD or tape, and there are plenty of them available. By all means buy one, or

Above: *Cupping ears to help locate birdsong. I know it looks daft, but you really can hear soft or distant noises much more clearly by doing this.*

several. But I know from my own experience that there is a limit to how much they will help. When I was planning a trip to North America in spring, I bought a tape of Yankee warblers and listened to it regularly, but believe me when I was out there in the woods their songs suddenly became a confusing cacophony – albeit a reasonably pleasant one. It was only when I concentrated on each song "live", and saw the singer, that I began to make the connections.

THE LANGUAGE OF BIRDS

Actually, being in those American woods reminded me how challenging getting to know songs and calls really is in the early days. The first lesson I had to relearn – and I pass it on to you – is that many – perhaps most – birds make several types of noise. Each noise is for a different purpose, and it is fascinating to learn the "language". Let me give an example that you've probably heard, even if you may not be totally aware of it.

Here is a selection of the noises made by a Blackbird, and their meanings.

Song: A lovely rich warbling. Lots of variety. Used by the male to advertise his territory and to attract a mate.

Alarm call: "Chink chink chink". Denotes danger, a warning that predators are nearby. Also often heard at dusk when the birds are about to go to roost.

Below: *The calls of young birds are very hard to identify. Many of them, like these fledgling Wrens, simply make a rather pathetic little squeak, which in fact seems rather appropriate for their age.*

Above: *When you hear the frantic "chink chink" of Blackbirds, chances are there is danger lurking. Maybe a domestic Cat, a hawk, or an owl (which is probably just trying to have a peaceful nap). The Blackbird's is one of the clearest alarm calls in nature.*

Right: *Blackbirds generally sing from a conspicuous position on top of a tree or roof, but now and then they sing in flight.*

Above: *Reed Warbler camouflaged in reeds. One of the birds that you are more likely to hear than to see – it has a very distinctive song. Generally, it does stick to reedbeds, along with two or three other brown warblers with equally distinctive songs.*

Distress call: A thin plaintive piping. The bird may have lost its young to, for example, a Grey Squirrel or a domestic Cat.
Flight call: "Tseep". Used by flying birds to keep in touch with each other.

They make other noises too, and most birds have a similar repertoire, so there really is a lot to learn.

NOISES DRAW ATTENTION

Why learn birdsong? Well, there are several reasons. A bird may be hidden in bushes, woodland, or reeds; the only way you may even know it is there is its song. Your attention may be drawn to birds flying way up overhead, for example, wild geese calling.

Above: *A Red Kite gliding silently overhead would be easy to miss if it weren't for the frantic cawing of the crows 'seeing it off'.*

Below: *A Stonechat and Meadow Pipits 'mobbing' a Short-eared Owl that probably just wanted a nap. Mind you, Short-eared Owls do often hunt by day, so maybe the smaller birds are right not to trust it.*

Distress calls may lead you to other birds. For example, crows cawing or gulls screeching as they mob a large bird of prey. Blackbirds and other small birds giving alarm calls and "scolding" may be because they have discovered a roosting owl. So may you!

IDENTIFICATION

This especially applies in the UK, where we have several species that look so similar (often the notorious "little brown jobs") that they are best identified by song or call. For example, Chiffchaff and Willow Warbler look almost identical (see pages 16-17), but have totally different songs.

Indeed, the Chiffchaff was named after its monotonous song – "chiff-chaff" – whilst the Willow Warbler has a lovely, wistful, cascading song. They could hardly sound more different. Wild geese and waders are two other families within which several species look very similar. The calls are the easiest way to tell them apart, and are, in fact, quite often the reason that you noticed the birds in the first place, as they often fly above or away from you. Wild geese and waders often look very much the same, and the calls are the easiest way to tell them apart.

You should trust your field guide to point out when a call or song is important

Above: *Green Sandpiper (above) and Wood Sandpiper (below). These two look very similar, but their calls are completely different. Wood calls "chif-if-if", whilst Green Sandpiper utters a liquid, rather panicky-sounding "tweet weet weet!", which may not look very distinctive written down, but is when you hear it.*

and indeed in some cases how to listen for them.

AESTHETIC

The final reason for becoming aware of bird noises is surely aesthetic. Quite simply, bird song can be absolutely delightful, and the calls can be incredibly atmospheric.

The person who coined the phrase "silent spring" to encapsulate the potential horror of losing our song birds to persecution and pollution surely got it spot on. Imagine a world without bird songs and calls. A sad place indeed.

Finally, take heart if you are still feeling apprehensive about sorting it all out.

Believe me, I know experienced birders whose visual identification skills are impressive, but who confess to having a blind spot – or rather a deaf ear – when it comes to sorting out calls and songs. But they still manage to be pretty good birders. Nevertheless, they don't simply ignore bird songs and calls, and neither should you. Just enjoy the sound – even if you don't know what's making it. But I bet you'll want to find out!

Left: People often rave about the dawn chorus, but there is another burst of song just before sundown. This dusk chorus can be just as impressive, and you don't have to get up early to hear it.

FINDING BIRDS

YOUR LOCAL PATCH

Indeed, your own backyard or garden may well be your local patch, but birdwatchers generally choose something a little more elaborate. My own patch is Hampstead Heath, and it fulfills the criteria pretty well. It has a mixed variety of habitats – woodland, hedges, open fields, some areas of water, and even a small reedbed. Also – and perhaps most exciting to me – it has Parliament Hill, which overlooks London and seems to lie on some kind of migration

Top: *Tottenham Marshes. A mixture of habitats in a small area is an ideal 'local patch'.*

Above: *River habitat. River valleys often act as avian motorways for migrating birds.*

Opposite right: *Great Crested Grebe. Now common over much of Britain, thanks to bird protection laws and lots of flooded gravel pits and reservoirs. A delight to birdwatchers and non-birdwatchers.*

route, so that in spring and autumn the birding can vary greatly from day to day, as warblers, swallows and martins, pipits, thrushes, etc pass through or over on their various migratory journeys. Every now and then I see a local rarity – remember anything that is new for your local patch is rare – but the greatest satisfaction is in keeping a record over the years and realizing that no two years are ever the same. There are certainly more productive patches than the Heath (and some less so as well, I imagine) but wherever you live you can bet there will be somewhere worth watching. A park, allotments, a stretch of canal – even or indeed especially in an urban area – a local reservoir or gravel pits, a river valley in suburbia or in the country, right up to an estuary, headland or island on the coast. I don't want to go on about it, but I really do think that any birdwatcher who hasn't done at least a bit of "patch work" has really missed something.

FINDING YOUR OWN BIRDS – WHERE TO LOOK AND WHEN

One of the most valuable skills – or is it an instinct? – that a birdwatcher can possess is recognizing a good bird place. Of course, experience is the key to it all. It's something you will inevitably practise on a relatively small scale on your local patch. For example, I recall even on my

very first visit to Hampstead Heath, I could anticipate which areas certain birds would prefer. Most obviously, I would expect wildfowl on the ponds, but even within these areas there were preferences. The deeper open water for diving ducks, like Tufted and Pochard; the shallower edges for dabblers, like Mallard; the shady banks for Moorhens, and so on. Where there are overhanging branches and a few reeds, that's where I'd expect Great Crested Grebes to nest – and they do. In fact, knowing what you expect (or at least hope) to see in a certain type of habitat is the very essence of efficient birdwatching. Wherever you go, you should be thinking: "What kind of birds like this kind of habitat?" You should almost assume that they are there somewhere, and make a point of trying to find them. Back on the Heath, for example, I would search the mature woodland trees for woodpeckers, Treecreepers, Nuthatches and tits – and most days that's exactly where I find them. The hedgerows are more favoured by Blackbirds, Song Thrushes and Dunnocks, and in summer by warblers such as Whitethroats and Blackcaps. On the short grassed playing fields, I'd expect gulls in winter, especially if the ground has become soggy. In spring and autumn the same fields may attract migrant Wheatears or pipits, while on the scattered perches

Left: Each bird in its place. Whinchat and Red-backed Shrike on isolated perches. Wheatears hopping on the rocks, Hobby in the air. They are on real heath here, but I have seen them all at Hampstead Heath, almost in the middle of London.

73

Above: *Urban allotments. As well as breeding birds, migrants often use allotments to 'refuel'. They can be particularly lively places during spring and autumn migration.*

of dock or thistles I'd look for Whinchats or Stonechats. Neither are common in Hampstead, but when they do occur I can accurately predict where they will be.

But few – perhaps no – birdwatchers can live on their local patch alone. You will inevitably want to go travelling and seek out new places and new birds. The principle, however, is the same – certain types of habitat or terrain will attract particular types of birds, and wherever you visit, you should be aware of what you "expect" to see.

Fortunately, these days there are masses of excellent books available on "where to watch birds" either in Britain and Ireland, or much more locally. Nearly all regions or counties have a "where to watch" guide. So buy these, read them, choose your locations, and prepare for the trip by checking on the area's specialities. The text of a good field guide will also keep reminding you of each species' habitat preferences.

All I am going to do here is list a variety of some of the more productive habitats, with a few notes on birding techniques, which I hope will help you make the most of your visit. It may also help you to recognize potentially good bird areas when you are exploring for yourself.

IN TOWN

It is a total fallacy to assume that there aren't many birds in urban areas. The very fact that there so much is built up means that bird-friendly oases act as magnets. It is probably easier to anticipate the good places in town than it is in the countryside. It is certainly easier to define and decide on a local patch in or near urban areas. Try gardens, especially those with a good variety of native trees and shrubs. Parks, especially those with lakes, and particularly if there is a dog and people-free area, possibly fenced off and designated as an urban nature reserve. Also allotments and cemeteries. Canals and river banks not only attract waterbirds but also often act as migration routes for small birds, as do high places, such as Parliament Hill near where I live in London. These can be fantastic viewpoints for visible migration. Keep looking up! It's amazing how many birds fly high – often unnoticed – over towns and cities. You can see everything from Cormorants and geese to migrating swallows, martins and Swifts. Swifts of course actually prefer buildings to nest in, as do Kestrels and Pied Wagtails. There is also an increasing number of rooftop gull colonies, even in totally landlocked cities,

and – ironically perhaps – rubbish tips attract huge numbers of gulls and gull watchers. Many of Britain's rarest gulls have been recorded on "dumps". British Black Redstarts after the Second World War became addicted to bomb sites and they still prefer derelict urban areas.

Below: *Kestrel. Another bird that is happy on the artificial cliff faces and ledges of buildings.*

Bottom: *Black Redstart. On the Continent, they breed in rocky terrain. Derelict sites, power stations and warehouses are their British home.*

Left: *Swifts in flight. The 'screaming' of Swifts is one of the characteristic sounds of summer, and is a wild noise over the middle of a city. They usually arrive in early May to nest under the roofs of houses.*

GRAVEL PITS AND RESERVOIRS

Probably the favourite local patches amongst birders and they are possibly the most birded type of habitat overall. They are good value since they not only attract the expected water birds, but also seem to act as a magnet to passing migrants in spring and autumn. Moreover, the bird

Left: *Walthamstow Reservoirs. These concrete reservoirs are much like the one that I studied when I was a lad. Definitely most productive in winter.*

Below: *Flooded gravel pit. Many gravel companies work with local wildlife trusts to create nature reserves when the pits are no longer in operation.*

Above: *An east wind and thundery weather in May. Ideal conditions for Black Terns – probably on their way to breed in Holland – to get 'displaced' over British reservoirs. They may stay for only a few minutes, so you have to be there at the right time.*

population will change with the seasons. The bleaker waters tend to be at their best during the winter, when ducks flock together and there is an influx of extra birds from the continent. More sheltered areas – particularly disused gravel pits – especially if they have reedbeds, tend to be at their most entertaining during spring, summer and autumn, with the additional attractions of dragonflies and aquatic plants and flowers. The fact is though that such areas offer all-year value. Two tips: a telescope is definitely essential at a big reservoir, and do walk round till you get the sun behind you.

ESTUARIES AND COASTAL MARSHES

These are splendidly prolific areas for birds, offering such spectacles as huge flocks of wild geese in winter, or a variety of migrant waders in spring and autumn. Fortunately, nowadays a large number of such places are official nature reserves. Mind you, the downside to that is that there are relatively few such areas left round our coasts that have not been developed and degraded. The ones that remain are havens for wildlife only because they are officially protected. But let's be grateful that they exist, and, what's more, they do offer all the viewing facilities of an official reserve. My main tips here are – yet again – get that sun behind you. Waders and wildfowl are challenging enough to sort out, without making it more difficult by squinting into the sun at them. Also, check the tide tables. Mudflats at low tide can be dauntingly vast and bleak, and indeed appear relatively birdless, but as the tide comes in birds

Left: *Knot and Dunlins, high-tide roost flock at Snettisham RSPB Reserve in north Norfolk. It's worth checking to find out which are the best tides for seeing really spectacular numbers.*

Below: *Brent Geese. Winter visitors in increasing numbers to estuaries and coastal marshes. Their distant calls sound like a huge pack of yapping dogs.*

will be concentrated in ever more densely packed flocks. If the tide gets really high, they may then fly off to inaccessible and unviewable offshore sandbanks, rocks, or saltmarshes. As the tide begins to fall, they will return to feed as soon as the first strips of mud are exposed, and this is another excellent time to see them. Flocks of waders flying to and from their roosts are amongst the world's great bird spectacles. Clouds of birds, constantly changing shape (the clouds I mean, not the birds). It seems amazing that they don't sometimes collide. And the sounds! You can literally hear the swoosh of wings as the birds wheel past or overhead. This is a good opportunity to get to know calls and wing patterns, but mainly just to enjoy the spectacle.

Below: A typical estuary selection. Gulls, waders and wildfowl. You soon appreciate which species prefer which areas: soft mud, sand, pebbles or shallow water. Take your time to scan, and make sure you see everything that there is to see.

SEA CLIFFS AND
SEABIRD ISLANDS

Once again, the fact is that there aren't that many big seabird colonies that aren't official reserves, so finding them and accessing them is easy enough. Do be aware though that cliffs that are teeming with life during the summer breeding season are literally birdless in winter. The only other note of caution I will add is: do be careful. I have seen people taking ridiculous risks leaning over precipices to get a better view. This is particularly dangerous when you are looking through binoculars or a camera, when you can easily lose your sense of how close to the edge you are.

"Where to Watch" books will tell you exactly where to go, what to expect to see and the best times to visit.

We're very lucky in the UK to have some of the best seabird spectacles in the world.

Left: *Seabird colony. It is not so much the large variety of species, but the sheer numbers of birds that can be almost overwhelming. Again, take your time and make sure that you appreciate the behaviour of individuals and pairs, feeding, fighting, grooming, and so on.*

Above: *Auks. Guillemots, Razorbills and Puffins are the Northern Hemisphere equivalent of penguins. But auks can fly, and in winter these pinnacles would be deserted.*

Below: *Bass Rock, Firth of Forth, Scotland. During the breeding season, it is literally turned white by thousands of Gannets, and their droppings. You can't land there – not enough room! – but the Seabird Centre at North Berwick, offers a unique viewing experience, with remote-control cameras.*

HEADLANDS, PROMONTORIES, AND SMALL ISLANDS

These are not only good for seabirds in summer, but areas that jut out from the coast are often excellent for seeing migrant birds of all kinds in spring and autumn. Mind you, it can be a very hit and miss affair. The weather conditions – especially wind direction – can make all the difference. For example, an east wind in October, especially with some mist or drizzle, can blow literally thousands of birds from the continent onto the British east coast. I have been lucky enough to be in north Norfolk or in Shetland at such a time, when every tree, bush, fence or even pathway was alive with Robins, thrushes and warblers. It is times like this that birdwatchers literally dream about! You feel suspended between exhilaration and panic. You know that anything might turn up, but you don't know where to look first. You may be faced with a choice: do you do your own thing and risk missing some good birds – but maybe find some of your own – or do you follow Birdline, or your pager, and/or the crowds? It's up to you. There is no right or wrong about it! In any event, it should be pretty exciting and possibly frustrating too – but that's birding!

Left: *Pallas's Warbler. A little gem from Siberia. It used to be very rare, with only 20 in Britain during 1896-1966, but there has been on average nearly 80 per year recently. More birds, or more birdwatchers?*

Above: *Abbey Pool, Tresco, Isles of Scilly. Rather a grand background to this glorified puddle, which has provided a temporary home for several rare American waders.*

Above: *Land's End and the west coast of Cornwall. Imagine a tiny migrant getting blown across the Atlantic and arriving at the very tip of England.*

Below: *Bluethroat (juvenile). A spring or autumn visitor, but this one is in autumn as it is in juvenile plumage, without the usual Union Jack waistcoat.*

SEAWATCHING

This is another activity available from headlands and islands. It is a pretty specialized form of birdwatching and I'm not sure I would recommend it for a beginner! It can be exciting, but then again it can be bewildering or indeed incredibly tedious! Basically, seawatchers sit looking out to sea through their bins or scopes and look for seabirds flying past offshore. Again, weather conditions make a huge difference, as does the time of the year. An onshore wind in autumn is probably the optimum situation. April and May can also be good. On good days, there can be an impressive passage: hundreds maybe thousands of Gannets, gulls, auks, wildfowl and hopefully – the seawatcher's main quarries – skuas, shearwaters and petrels. When this happens it is certainly thrilling, but it is also a big test of your identification skills. Birds are often some way out and the conditions can be unpleasant: wet and windy. You may well decide it's all a bit more than you

Left: *Cape Clear Island, southwest Ireland. Famous for the huge number of seabirds seen flying past its southern headlands.*

Below: *Gannets are big and nice and easy to spot.*

can manage! My advice would be that if you happen to be at a seawatching location and there is a bunch of birders staring out to sea, ask them if there is much action. "Anything happening?" is the usual enquiry. If the answer is "yes", make yourself cozy on the end of the line, and have a go. Listen to what's being said. Someone will invariably be giving a running commentary and calling out directions. "Red-throated Diver flying past the blue buoy at 3 o'clock." The latter refers to direction, not the time! Imagine you are the centre of a clock and 12 o'clock is directly in front of you. So 3 o'clock is some way to the right. Don't be discouraged if at first you seem to miss more than you see. And don't be shy about asking. Equally, if you find it all a bit more stressful than enjoyable, don't be afraid to pack it in and try something easier! By the way, early morning tends to be the best time for seawatching, with a possible resurgence in the late afternoon, and be sure to be prepared for that unexpected squall.

Below: Seabirds at sea. All are sitting close inshore on calm water. It can happen, but more often than not they are racing past half a mile away, or more.

PELAGICS

This is seawatching for the more adventurous, and those with a steady stomach.

The RSPB and other groups organize boat trips – for example, from Bridlington in Yorkshire or off the coast of Cornwall – which get you out where seabirds really belong – on the ocean. Beware though that this by no means guarantees that you will find many – or indeed any – birds. I'll just say that pelagics can be fantastic, or total nightmares. Either way, they are likely to be memorable so – as ever – my advice is go and try one. (You don't mind if I don't come with you though, do you?)

Left: *Pelagic birds at sea. Pelagos means sea (in Greek), and it is undeniably an exciting experience to be out there, where the birds belong, and to realize what an extraordinarily harsh life they lead.*

Below: *Seawatchers brave all weathers, so don't forget to wrap up warm!*

WOODLAND

Another habitat where early morning is certainly the best time to be out, if only to enjoy the dawn chorus, undiluted by the sounds of distant traffic and aeroplanes. Woodland birds are more vocal and active in the early hours, and therefore easier to hear and see, as they are more likely to be flitting around looking for food. It is the sound that will catch your attention (this is where it really helps to get to know songs and calls) and it is movement that will attract your eye. Woodland watching is inevitably easier when the air is calm and the leaves aren't rustling and shimmering. But remember, even on a windy day, leaves rarely float upwards! A bird that may be invisible in the treetops will suddenly become obvious when it flits from branch to branch (or maybe flies up and away).

Left: *Redwing. A winter thrush that is addicted to red berries. A flock of Redwings can strip a cotoneaster tree in no time.*

Above: *Garden Warbler on the edge of woodland. One of those secretive warblers that you can often hear but not see singing from deep within a bush.*

Also, think like a bird. The vast majority of a woodland bird's daytime activity is to do with display (including singing) or feeding. A bird in song is likely to be static and therefore hard to spot, so you need to follow your ear, as it were. On many occasions, the singer may in fact be on a fairly conspicuous perch – a bare branch or even the very top of a tree. So try scanning the likely song perches. Calling birds are more likely to be on the move, foraging for food. The calls themselves take experience to sort out (many of them are soft and very similar "tsips" and "seesees") but fortunately the movements are likely to catch your eye. And think what the birds are feeding on, and search accordingly. Trees with berries

are likely to attract Blackbirds and thrushes. Insect eaters seek out sunny patches, where flies are most likely to swarm. The edge of the wood, where the sunlight hits the outer trees is the best and easiest place to look for warblers and flycatchers. Some birds seem to be almost addicted to certain trees. Siskins and Redpolls love alders and birches. Again, a good field guide will point you in the right direction.

Woodlands can sometimes seem strangely empty. At around midday things often go very quiet, as birds rest and preen. In mid-winter the birds flock together more (for safety and efficiency of searching) and it's all too easy to fail to connect with them. Late summer can seem deadest of all, though ironically there may be more birds in the woods than at any other time. However, newly fledged youngsters are hiding from potential predators and keeping very quiet, and the adults are also keeping a low profile while they moult into fresh plumage.

Nevertheless, a good morning in a woodland can be truly magical. The secret is get up early, move slowly and quietly, and take your time. I am personally not convinced that birding in groups is the best way to work a woodland, but – having said that – dawn chorus walks are extremely popular, and I have never met any one who has been on one and didn't thoroughly enjoy it.

Left: *Mistle Thrush singing. Mistle Thrushes often start singing very early in the year – even in midwinter – almost invariably from the very top of a tall tree.*

Right: Siskin on hazel. They also love alders and birches. Addicted to catkins? They can also be seen feeding on nut bags in your garden.

Below: Foraging tit flock. Other species will often tag along, including Treecreepers, Goldcrests and Nuthatches. Food finding is much more efficient in a flock, and there is safety in numbers.

MOORLAND AND MOUNTAIN

Exploring this kind of habitat is likely to be as much hiking and trekking as birding. It's good for you, even if you don't see much! In winter, the uplands can be literally birdless, but in summer there are certain specialities that are definitely worth searching for, be it Ptarmigan and Dotterel in the Cairngorms, Golden Eagles in the Highlands, or Ring Ouzels and Golden Plover on the moors. Be prepared for a lot of walking and possibly bad weather, and make sure you know where you are, where you're going, and how to get back. The birds may not always "perform", but now and again you will have a really memorable day out, in an atmosphere that is totally unique, and a complete contrast to, say, the teeming activity at a seabird colony, or the teeming birdwatchers at a coastal reserve!

Left: *Dotterel can be hard to find on their mountain-top breeding grounds, but, if you do, they can be tame.*

Above: *Golden Plover. On the breeding grounds you could see their parachuting display flight.*

Opposite inset: *Ring Ouzel. Sometimes known as the 'Mountain Blackbird', its mournful song literally echoes around the ravines.*

OTHER LOCATIONS –
AND GENERAL RULES

I can't stress it enough: different habitats attract different birds. Whether you are looking to add to your day list or your life list, the secret is to visit as many types of terrain as possible, not only those I have already suggested. There are others that have their specialities: for example,

Below: *Crested Tit. Another one that in Britain you will find only north of the Border, and yet they also live in the southern Mediterranean region.*

Opposite Right: *Caledonian Forest, Scotland is perfect habitat for Crested Tit and Capercaillie.*

Opposite Below: *A male Capercaillie is as big as a Turkey, and yet I have never seen one. And, believe me, I've tried! Alas, they are getting scarcer in the Caledonian Forests of Scotland.*

the ancient conifer forests of Scotland for Capercaillie, Crested Tit and Scottish Crossbill; the oak woods of Wales for Pied Flycatchers, Redstarts and Wood Warblers; the heathlands of Dorset for Nightjars and Dartford Warblers, and many more.

I have tried to show their magic on my TV series, and there are many books to tell you more. By all means buy and use them, but one final suggestion: make sure you do a bit of exploring for yourself. It is ever so satisfying to discover a good bird spot, and even better to find a good bird on it!

Above: *Redstart. Birdwatchers in ancient times used to believe that Redstarts lost their red tails and became Robins in winter. They are in fact summer visitors to Britain.*

Right: *Pied Flycatcher. A summer visitor. This is a female, and the dapper little black-and-white males contrast wonderfully with the soft green shades of a Welsh oakwood.*

Above: *Red Kite country, near Tregaron, Wales. Another of those diminishing habitats whose very existence depends upon protection by conservation bodies.*

Right: *Dartford Warbler. Presumably so named because it was first identified in Kent. Dorset is now its stronghold, but its range is spreading.*

BIRD RESERVES

I can't think of a better way to get turned on to birds than to visit a major bird or nature reserve. This is birdwatching made easy – and all the more enjoyable for it. OK, reserves vary – some are more impressive than others, and even the best can have their off days – but if you have a good experience it may well hook you for life. The huge advantage is that these places are laid out and managed both for the birds and for the birdwatchers. The RSPB, a Wildlife Trust, or some such conservation body, creates and maintains optimum conditions to attract and concentrate the birds, and provides ideal viewing conditions. A typical day out involves following clear sign posts to the car park, near which there will probably be an information centre (selling everything from field guides and binoculars to souvenirs, and quite possibly food and drink). There will also be a "what's about" board, kept up to date with the most recent sightings. An information leaflet, or displays and sign posts, or instructions from the reserve staff will make sure you take the right trails and pathways and visit the best hides.

Below: *The RSPB reserve at Loch Garten was originally created to protect a single pair of Ospreys, the first that had bred in Britain for many years. Nowadays, Ospreys are relatively common in Scotland, and are beginning to breed in England and Wales. A success story indeed.*

HIDES

Nature reserve hides are not like photographic hides (i.e. canvas boxes or tiny garden sheds). some of them are more like grandstands. They offer shelter from inclement weather and a great view of the birds. Even the biggest ones can get full on a busy day and you may even have to wait your turn. It goes without saying that people should be relatively quiet in a hide, as sometimes the birds are extremely close, but don't shut up altogether! I have often seen beginners staring through their bins and rummaging through their field guides, clearly a bit fazed by a possibly bewildering variety of new birds. A simple rule: don't be afraid to ask. Chances are there will either be other people equally puzzled, who will be positively relieved to discover that they aren't the only ones. And there will almost

Above: *Avocet. The logo of the RSPB, and a bird that almost symbolizes the success of bird reserves. Create the right conditions, and the birds arrive almost immediately.*

Below: *Minsmere is arguably Britain's best known and most popular reserve. One morning I saw and heard over 100 species there before 6am.*

certainly be someone more expert who will be delighted to sort things out (we all love to show off a bit). There may even be a reserve warden on hand who will give you a running commentary and probably a potted history of the reserve as well. It is part of their job and some of them are brilliant at it.

A few bits of hide advice: if there are a number of hides on several sides of the reserve – for example, surrounding a large lake or scrape – it's worth walking round and getting the sun behind you. This seems obvious I know, but I have often seen people squinting at unidentifiable silhouettes, when a short walk would reveal a nicely backlit picture in revealing full colour.

In a hide, a telescope really comes into its own. You can set it up, nice and steady, on the window ledge (you may not even need a tripod) and get amazing close up views. Also, use it to scan – you may spot birds you didn't even realize were there. And that's another rule: take your time. All too often, I have seen people nip into a hide and ask: "What's about?", tick off the immediately visible birds, and leave after only a few minutes. On more than one occasion the moment they've gone,

something good has flown in and they've missed it. Birds come and go all the time, especially at lakes and estuaries, so give yourself half an hour, rather than half a minute.

Mind you, my final piece of hide advice is: don't stay in there too long. The view through hide windows is often terrific, but it is also limited. You can't see what's above or behind you. I have told this salutary tale before, but it illustrates a point. I was at Minsmere one morning, walking along a path through the reedbeds, when I spotted six distant dots flying towards me from way down the coast. As they got closer I realized they were Spoonbills. To my delight, they flew right above my head and circled high over the main scrape. But they didn't land. For some reason they glided on and away, until I lost them over the horizon. Nevertheless, I'd had a terrific view, lacking only the extra pleasure of sharing it with other birders. But maybe I could. At that moment, the door of the nearby hide opened and two birdwatchers emerged. "Hey! What about those Spoonbills!?" I enthused. They looked puzzled and more than a little deflated. "Er … what Spoonbills?"

But then again that's birdwatching: you can't win 'em all.

Above: *Spoonbills flying over – a terrific view.*

Opposite: *Spoonbills feeding. The sort of close-up view you would probably only get from a hide. On the other hand, they may just fly straight over.*

Right: *Inside a hide. A chance to chat to other birdwatchers, of all ages and levels of expertise.*

TWITCHING

The media now use the word "twitcher" to refer to any and all birdwatchers. This is as inaccurate as saying that all sprinters are athletes, therefore all athletes are sprinters! Strictly speaking, twitching is a very specific and somewhat extreme kind of birding. It is rarity hunting. It is also often mass birding, when crowds of hundreds, sometimes even thousands, gather at one place to tick off a rare bird that they already know has been found (and they hope is still there!) In a sense, therefore, twitching is the very antithesis of what I personally feel is the essence of birding: unpredictability, the fact that you never really know what you are going to see. If you go twitching, you know exactly what you are going to see (or at least hope you are going to see!). The fact is, it may have flown off. Arguably, this adds to the excitement, though it also means that twitching can be a frenetic and stressful activity. Indeed the derivation of the word indicates this. It was coined many years ago to describe a bunch of early twitchers who supposedly became so overexcited at the prospect of seeing a new bird, and so riddled with anxiety at the possibility of missing it, that they would literally shake, tremble or "twitch" with the emotion of the whole thing!

I'll be honest, twitching is not really my bag – as we used to say back in the sixties, when I did a bit of twitching, and proved to myself that I really couldn't stand the strain – but, I assure you, I have absolutely nothing against it. I would say that if rarity hunting becomes a total obsession, to the extent that you become oblivious to behaviour and beauty, then that's a bit sad. But I really don't think that even the most hardened twitcher is that far gone! The truth is, that most birders do a bit of twitching now and again. In fact, I would recommend that you try it. The information technology these days is simply fantastic. You can get bird news sent direct to your mobile. You can ring Birdline (national or local) and you will hear constantly updated news of rare birds, plus instructions of how to find them. Pagers are even more amazing: they even bleep or vibrate when a mega rarity is found, and you'll get a sort of running commentary on the little screen: "the bird is showing well ... the bird hasn't been seen for half an hour, etc, etc". And of course the Internet constantly updates news of rarities and scarcities from all over the world. So, if you fancy a weekend's twitching, why not? Choose a bird, and go for it! I will simply add a few more comments.

Above: *Crowds of this size are common when a rare bird is reported, even if it is a boring 'little brown job'. So, do you fancy this kind of birding? I confess that my personal answer is: "Not a lot." But I'd recommend that you do go on a twitch, and make up your own mind. It's an experience!*

DISADVANTAGES

Twitching can be expensive (on bird information bills and petrol) and time-consuming. You may spend more time on the road driving than birdwatching. You may find the big crowds positively claustrophobic (I do). You may not see the bird (twitchers call this "dipping out") and believe me this can be pretty upsetting (I've seen twitchers in tears!).

It is arguably a bit pointless (or premature) for a beginner. I guess I'm being a rather purist, but it is surely better to get

to know the commoner birds and birding techniques before going off rarity chasing. Rarities can wait. But then again can they? You may get news of an extreme rarity – a first for Britain perhaps – that may never turn up again in your lifetime, so why not go for it?

ADVANTAGES

You are more or less guaranteed to see some "good" birds, and there is an undeniable frisson about rarities. This is enhanced by the shared experience. It is rather nice to

share your joy if the bird is showing well (or your sorrow if it isn't!). In any event, the social side of twitching is – to me – arguably the most enjoyable side of it. I very rarely go twitching, but when I do I enjoy seeing friends and faces as much as the bird itself. It's certainly a consolation if the bird has flown.

What certainly is true is that twitching (in its true sense) is here to stay. So too are birdlines, pagers, texts and tweets. So why not take advantage of them, to whatever extent you choose? For example, I visit the London Bird Club website to keep up to date with what's going on, especially in my local area. If I have seen good local migration over the Heath, I like to hear whether or not other areas in the south-east have had similar experiences. I confess I have also rung Birdline to check out where *not* to go if I want to avoid the crowds!

A phenomenon I have noticed increasingly in recent years is birdwatchers that I certainly wouldn't call heavy twitchers using Birdline or their pagers or smartphones to give a shape to their weekend's birding. For example, one early October I was in north Norfolk. There was a big fall of migrant birds and a lot of possible locations to choose from. As it happens, I decided to do my own thing and try to find my own birds. However,

Left: *Boarding boats at St Agnes, Isles of Scilly. Chasing rarities around this rare-bird Mecca can be frustrating. You can't be on several islands at the same time, and you can, quite literally, miss the boat.*

Above: *On your marks, get set, go! Racing for a rarity? Well, twitchers have been known to leap overboard before the boat docks, and then wade – or swim! – to get there first. Honestly!*

as I explored the coastline, I kept meeting people who were letting their pagers dictate their itineraries. They followed the latest news up and down the coast from one rarity to another. Some they saw, some they didn't, but generally they seemed to be having a thoroughly good time, and the hit and miss element seemed to be adding to the fun rather than the frustration. I think! Personally, I'm sure I couldn't have stood the strain! What's more, the kudos and thrill of finding my own rarity and putting it on the pager appeals to my vanity. But each to his or her own. I stress again, the technology is in place, thousands of people

enjoy twitching now and again, so for heaven's sake give it a try. Being a child of the seventies (well, a 30-year-old of the seventies actually), I quote that well known hippy maxim: "whatever turns you on". I'm talking about birding of course.

I would just, however, like to repeat my grumble about the media using the word (and image) of twitching as if that is what birdwatching is all about. It's not only inaccurate, it's also potentially off-putting. I mean, I somehow can't imagine too many non-birdwatchers seeing the scene opposite and thinking: "Oh, that looks fun. I wish I were there."

Right: *Golden-winged Warbler. A very attractive little bird and also, arguably, one of the most unexpected rarities ever to reach Britain. They are not common, even in North America where they breed. This one, found in early February 1989, should have been wintering in Nicaragua, Panama, Colombia or thereabouts. Instead, it ended up in the car park of a suburban supermarket in Kent.*

Below: *Still generally accepted as Britain's biggest twitch: on the Golden-winged Warbler's first day alone, at least 2,000 twitchers wandered the nearby streets and peered into back gardens. Heaven knows how many people travelled to Larkfield to 'tick off' the bird during its two-month stay. The event was, of course, widely featured in the media. I'm not sure how the local people felt about the invasion, but no doubt the supermarket did a roaring trade.*

THE BIRDING YEAR

As I have already mentioned, particular places are best at particular times of the year. Some habitats – such as moorland and seabird islands – can literally be almost birdless during the winter, yet teeming with life during the summer. It obviously follows that, before you visit an area, it's worth checking which is its best season in one of those 'where to watch birds' books. It is all too easy to make a mistake, as I realized when a South African friend of mine visited the UK and decided to take a few days off in Scotland. Just before he set off, he phoned me with a request: "Bill, where's the best place to see a Puffin?" "In the middle of the Atlantic," was my discouraging reply. Had it been summer, I could have been more optimistic, but it was then late November, when most British Puffins are indeed way out at sea. Instead, I directed him to some of the best wild geese sites in Scotland (which of course, as it happens, would have been gooseless in summer). Alas, we can't have everything.

Above: *Turtle Doves. A quintessential sound of summer: the soft 'purring' of Turtle Doves. Alas, it's becoming scarcer.*

It's all to do with migration of course. Birds fly north to breed, or south to winter. Some travel vast distances, others may simply shift a few miles, probably between higher breeding grounds to less-harsh areas near the coast. These movements and changes not only mean that the travelling birdwatcher is likely to choose 'seasonal' destinations, but they are also what make some truly productive areas worth visiting throughout the year. To put it simply, instead of you going to the birds, the birds come to you; and each season will bring different species.

To show you what I mean, we asked artist Dave Daly to create a sort of ideal 'dream patch', and, on the following pages, he shows how it would change throughout the year: an artwork equivalent to time-lapse photography. To me, this is a delightful way to demonstrate just how wonderful the fluidity of the bird population is. I hope that you agree.

Above: *Wryneck. A classic 'semi rarity' that you hope to see at migration time at one of those coastal hotspots. Related to the woodpeckers. The name refers to the way that the bird can twist and turn its head and neck.*

Left: *Waxwings. In some winters, hundreds – even thousands – invade Britain from Scandinavia. Other years there are virtually none. In a 'waxwing year', check out any red berries, even in gardens and cities.*

WINTER

JANUARY, FEBRUARY AND EARLY MARCH

It may feel chilly to us, but to many north European birds the British winter is positively balmy. Flocks of wild geese and swans visit us from both the east (Russia and Siberia) and the northwest (Greenland and Iceland). Likewise, many of the ducks on the lake are likely to be from eastern Europe or beyond, rather than from within Britain. Grey Herons are conspicuous at this time of year, whilst flocks of Lapwings and Golden Plovers may number several hundreds. Winter thrushes (Redwings and Fieldfares) have already gobbled up most of the berries, and have resorted to feeding on the ground, whilst tits find seeds in the reedbed. The bird perched on the barbed wire is a Great Grey Shrike: a rare winter visitor likely to attract a twitch when news gets out.

SPRING

LATE MARCH, APRIL AND MAY

The main feature is the arrival of the 'summer visitors' (even if they do arrive in spring). Chiffchaff and Wheatear are likely to be amongst the earliest. The scene shown here is likely to be late April, as there's also a Cuckoo, a Sedge Warbler, a Swift and several Swallows. Amongst resident species, breeding is already well underway. The Lapwing flocks have broken up into pairs. Great Crested Grebe and Dabchick (Little Grebe) are both in breeding plumage, as is a male Reed Bunting (in the reeds!), now with a smart black head rather than the duller stripes of winter. Meanwhile, the last small party of Whooper Swans is heading off northwest to their nesting places in Greenland or Iceland, which should just be beginning to defrost.

SUMMER

JUNE AND JULY

A time that is often ignored by some birdwatchers, but which can be particularly delightful as there are young birds around, such as the family of Mute Swans. Some birds – such as the Curlews – that have bred up on the moorlands have already reared their young and are now forming flocks. This is a time of moult for many birds. Adults lose feathers that have become worn and broken by the rigours of raising families, whilst some young birds are growing adult-type feathers. The two Starlings (bottom right corner) are in 'half and half' plumage. The male Mallards by the water's edge will soon lose their colours and go into dull 'eclipse' plumage, when they look like the permanently brown females. The birds with the white wing bars are Black-tailed Godwits (great name!) A few breed in Britain, but it's just as likely that they are Arctic birds already on their way back south. The Sedge Warbler seems to have claimed this corner of the reedbed: it may well have a nest and young nearby.

AUTUMN

AUGUST AND SEPTEMBER

Once autumn migration gets underway, this is the season when the bird population can change literally overnight. It is worth visiting your patch day after day. The small waders with black bellies are Dunlins: all adults, which may indicate a poor breeding season, although generally the juveniles (they don't have black bellies) do travel later anyway. The Curlew-like birds (several of them snoozing) are in fact Whimbrels, which may have bred in the Northern Isles of Scotland. Perched in the foreground is a juvenile Whinchat, taking on 'fuel' before making an amazing journey down to Africa. Likewise, Swallow roosts build up in the reedbeds – sometimes, flocks may number thousands – before they finally set off south, mainly in late September. Most British Swallows spend our winter in South Africa.

LATE AUTUMN, EARLY WINTER

OCTOBER, NOVEMBER AND DECEMBER

And the year comes full circle. But before that, October: many birders' favourite month. There may be a few lingering summer migrants, but this is the time when winter visitors arrive. Wildfowl include Whooper Swans, and a flock of Barnacle Geese – in ancient times people believed that they summered under the sea and hatched from barnacle shells. The single Snow Goose may be a genuine wild bird, but is just as likely to be an 'escape' that has latched onto the Barnacle flock. Redwings and Fieldfares from Scandinavia are tucking into the hawthorn berries, and, nearby, there are a couple of tiny Goldcrests and, above them, a couple of Snow Buntings. These may indicate an influx of migrants from farther east: the Continent or even beyond. They may have been blown across to Britain by an east wind. 'Falls' of migrants often include something unusual. October is the rare-bird month. Ask any twitcher!

BROADEN YOUR HORIZONS

There is no doubt that going with an organized group, led by an expert, is an excellent way for a beginner to get to know something about birds, birdwatching and birdwatchers. In fact, it's certainly not just for beginners, and indeed a mix of abilities makes for a richer experience. One day outings are usually referred to as "field meetings" and may be run by a local RSPB group, bird club or wildlife trust. They may be local, or may involve a coach trip, perhaps to a nationally famous reserve. They are excellent experiences both ornithologically and socially. You may wish to take the principle further and go on a specialist birding holiday, either to a remoter part of Britain or abroad. Quite simply, you can go just about anywhere these days and watch birds, with the whole trip organized by a specialist tour operator who will book your travel and accommodation and provide an expert guide who will make sure you see everything there is to see. Such holidays really are terrific value. In fact, quite a few of the clients may not be birdwatchers at all, but simply people who enjoy a different way of seeing a country apart from the usual tourist route. So, read the adverts in the bird magazines, send for the brochures, and take your pick.

My only word of cautionary advice is that if you are a relative newcomer even to British birds, then stick with the UK for your first few expeditions. I have to admit that I have led trips – for example to Cyprus – where one or two of the group were constantly lagging behind and getting distracted by birds that they could see and probably had seen plenty of back home. I remember one day we had all trudged up a small mountain only to look behind and below us to see a lady in our party staring intently through her telescope at what we naturally assumed was something really special. We all literally ran back down to her. "What have you got?" I panted. "A Goldfinch. Isn't it pretty?" Well yes, it was but – and no disrespect to the lady or the Goldfinch – it wasn't exactly what we'd come to Cyprus to look for. We nearly made her carry us all back up the hillside to where someone else was now looking at

Opposite above: *Birdwatchers in the Negev desert. In the early morning, deserts can be surprisingly cool and blissfully peaceful, and alive with birds.*

Opposite below: *River Euphrates, Eastern Turkey. Go birding, and see historic sites at the same time.*

a Golden Oriole (which was the sort of bird we'd come to see!).

But there are no rules. If you want to go birding abroad with a group, then you can and should, although I would make this little suggestion: get to know your British birds reasonably well first, or else you just might find yourself lagging behind, and just possibly slightly irritating your companions.

You may, of course, decide to go it alone in foreign lands. The plus being that you certainly won't annoy fellow birders that way! The minus being that you may wonder where to look and what to look for. Fear not, yet again all the information is available. There are "Where to Watch" books for just about every country in the world, and you can even get trip reports from people who have been there before you. This is, of course, when you need to purchase that European field guide, or beyond. Most areas of the world now have excellent field guides. And there is an increasing number of international DVDs and CDs available from the specialist outlets. As they say … it's never been easier.

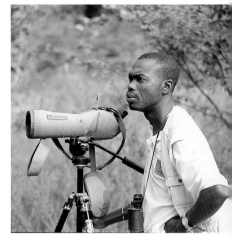

Above: *Local guides are often brilliant at spotting birds that, without their help, you wouldn't even have noticed.*

Right: *Lesser Flamingos; Lake Nakuru, Kenya. One of those sights you've probably seen on the telly, but there's nothing like the real thing.*

Below left: *Superb Starling, Kenya. That's its name, not just a description. No disrespect to 'our' Common Starling, but this one is more impressive.*

Below: *Red-billed Hornbill, Kenya. Birds are often particularly tame around the tourist lodges. In fact, I have enjoyed some of my best birding whilst lounging on a balcony sipping a cold drink.*

Above: *Bee-eater. A Mediterranean dazzler. In fact, it's a rare treat to see one perched like this. More often, you hear their bubbly calls from way overhead, where they are really hard to spot in the glare of a southern sky.*

Opposite: *Hoopoe. Probably the most striking and memorable bird of your first Mediterranean holiday. They never cease to delight birders and non-birders alike, especially when they fly, looking like huge, stripy butterflies. The name refers to its call: a monotonous "hoo hoo".*

I will also offer a wee bit of advice on family holidays, and this is born of personal experience. Don't forget that your wife, husband or children might not share your interest – or is it becoming an obsession? – in birds. Being dragged round a Spanish sewage farm to see Black-winged Stilts might not be the family's idea of the perfect holiday excursion. The secrets are moderation and organization, and getting up early, which is the best time for birding anyway, especially in hot countries. I get up at dawn and go for a morning walk or short drive, and I am usually back to join the family for a slightly late breakfast. I may take another hour or two's stroll in the late afternoon or early evening. Possibly, later in the week, I will negotiate a day out for a longer expedition to somewhere I have read about in the Where to Watch book. (There aren't as many official reserves in Europe, but they do exist.) And if my wife wants a day out (or a day off) then it's only fair to make sure she gets it. I have seen an awful lot of birds abroad on family holidays, and I am still very happily married! It can be done.

CONSERVATION

These days, everybody knows that birds – and other wildlife – are under threat. It is unarguable that many previously common species are diminishing in numbers. It is most obvious to someone of my age when I go for a walk in the British countryside. When I was a kid, back in the early 1950s, I did a lot of my birdwatching on farmland on the edge of Birmingham. In winter, I could expect to see flocks of Yellowhammers and Tree Sparrows, and in summer I would find Lapwings and Skylarks nesting in just about every field. If I visited the same farmland now I simply would not see those birds in such numbers. Some of them may have gone entirely. But it is not all doom and gloom. There are other species that have increased. Very often it is as a result of conservation and the management efforts of organizations such as the RSPB, the Wildlife Trusts, the Wildfowl and Wetlands Trust, Natural England, and other more local groups. In the context of this book, let me reassure you that there are still plenty of birds to watch!

However, I honestly believe that anyone who does enjoy watching birds is honour bound – and I'm sure would want – to help conserve and protect them. So how do you help? Really, it's quite simple – join something! The RSPB, your local county Wildlife Trust, if possible both or more. Your membership fee and your name on their campaigns are help enough. If you want to get more actively involved, there are lots of opportunities for volunteer work – everything from manning a reserve bookshop to digging ditches out on the marshes – which are not only invaluable, but also satisfying and fun.

In fact, I often think that instead of 'conservation', the key word these days should be 'creation'. There is a lovely film called Field of Dreams. It's actually about baseball. It involves a baseball fan (played by Kevin Costner) whose obsession with his long-gone heroes leads him to build a baseball park on the farm where he lives, in the apparently crazy hope that this will somehow bring the legendary players back to life. In his head, he continually hears an assuring voice telling him: "Build it, and they will come." He does, and they do. So what's that got to do with birds?

Opposite: *Male Hobby at nest. In recent years, these lovely falcons have bred in woodland near my home in London. Like most birds of prey, they are flourishing because of stricter controls over persecution and poisoning. But I was pretty amazed to find a Hobby's nest in such an urban area.*

Well, I reckon that catchphrase, motto – call it what you will – could equally apply to attracting wildlife to nature reserves. Except that we are talking reality, not movie dreamland.

The simple and sad fact is that there really aren't all that many truly natural areas left in Britain. So, the way forward is not so much saving existing habitats, as creating (or sometimes re-creating) new ones. This may involve reclaiming land – dry or wet – and completely transforming it. Fortunately, many industries these days are accepting their responsibilities to the environment (which they often adversely effect) and they are much more enlightened about returning land to a wilder state. Thus, disused mining areas, rubbish tips, shooting ranges, and particularly gravel diggings, have become nature reserves, made all the better by the expert management of such organisations as local wildlife trusts and the RSPB. I think it would be true to say that many of the species that are increasing in numbers are doing so because of the creation of favourable conditions at nature reserves.

For example, the Wildfowl and Wetlands centre at Barn Elms in London used to be four concrete-sided rectangular reservoirs. In fact, they weren't a bad place for diving ducks in winter and – because they were alongside the flyway of the River Thames – they attracted quite a good selection of passing migrants. But, be honest, you couldn't have called them exactly attractive, or indeed wild. Over recent years, however, the Wildfowl and Wetlands Trust has utterly re-landscaped the area, so that it now features lagoons of different depths, islands, reedbeds, and even a tidal inlet, all criss-crossed by walkways, and overlooked by hides. The whole place has been custom built to attract wildlife, and to provide wonderful viewing and educational facilities for visitors.

It may seem a tenuous link between Kevin Costner's baseball park and Barn Elms, but the motto could be the same: "Build it, and they will come."

What's more, you can be involved. There's bound to be a spot near you where your practical help will be appreciated.

GARDENS

Why not start close to home? You can make a valuable contribution to conservation merely by gardening in an environmentally friendly fashion. As it happens, gardens are one of the most productive habitats of all these days.

My own little plot in London is barely 15 metres square, but I have managed to find room for a couple of small ponds, at least half a dozen nest boxes, and an array of feeders offering everything from sunflower seeds and peanuts to live mealworms.

As I write, it is late February. If I look through my back window right now, it's a pretty lively scene. I can see a telltale splashing that tells me that the frogs are back in the ponds. A pair of Wood Pigeons is checking out last year's nesting tree, which I recently pruned, but took care to leave with thicker cover near the window sill where the pigeons usually build their flimsy bundle of twigs. By the rockery, a Jay has bullied his way to the front of the mealworm queue, whilst nearby a pair of Blackbirds, a Song Thrush and a Robin wait their turns. A couple of Dunnocks are shuffling amongst the snowdrops in the flowerbed, and an unseen Wren is blasting out its improbably loud song. On the seed feeders, there are Blue, Great, and Coal Tits, whilst a dazzling lemon-coloured male Siskin is dangling on the peanuts. I can also see a Goldcrest flitting around our solitary fir tree behind the shed, and I can hear the "si si si" of a little flock of Long-tailed Tits as they go rollicking through the willow (I have still never seen Long-tailed Tits on a feeder, but they have taken up this activity in some parts of England). In any case, the House Sparrows have just taken over. I do have five House Sparrows regularly in my garden. Alas, they are becoming quite a rarity these days. They have mysteriously almost disappeared from many of our cities. So, I am particularly pleased to see a pair with three of last year's youngsters, all looking fit and well fed. I'd like to think I've helped them through the winter.

So, that's not bad is it? Over a dozen species out there in my little garden at this very minute, and – with any luck – six or seven of them will stay on to breed. Imagine that happening in literally thousand of gardens across the country (and indeed the world!) and you can appreciate that it really

Right: *Corn Bunting. Let's face it, this is one of the least striking birds, and arguably a bit clumsy with it. But it does have a cheery little song that is often likened to the jangling of a bunch of keys. This used to be a very widespread and characteristic sound of British farmland, but, alas, this is another one that is becoming scarce. It's not so easy to manage a nature reserve to attract them, since they like – as their name implies – traditional fields of corn, especially barley.*

Below: *Lapwing. One of my favourite birds, either in flocks or as individuals. I often think that, if it were a rarity, a Lapwing would attract a huge twitch. Alas, they are definitely becoming less common owing to the pressures of modern, intensive, arable farming. Fortunately, they respond very well to specially created nature reserves.*

is an example of conservation in practice on a very grand scale.

So, at the very least, feed the birds and put up a couple of nest boxes. But if you fancy providing something more elaborate – and even more productive – there are some excellent books (not to mention the occasional television series!) that will tell you how to create everything from ponds and marsh gardens to wildflower meadows.

I can't resist saying it again: "Build it, and they will come!"

Above: *A bird-friendly garden. It's obviously the work of a wildlife lover with several different habitats. Don't worry if your patch is much smaller.*

Right: *Goldfinches on teasel heads. I know many gardeners hate the thistle family, but seed-eating birds love them. That's the key to good wildlife gardening: leave some of it messy. It's less work that way, too.*

BIRD FAIRS AND EVENTS

I've said before that if I were challenged to turn a non-birdwatcher on to birds I would take them on a trip to the seabird colonies of the Farne Islands. If – as an extension of that – I was asked to introduce them to the whole world of birdwatching, I would take them to the Bird Fair. When I say 'the' fair, I mean the incredible event that takes place on the third weekend of August every year at Rutland Water Nature Reserve. The first one was held in 1989 in – as I recall – a single, relatively small marquee. Nowadays, there are several massive marquees and several thousand visitors over the weekend, who come from all over the country and indeed the world. Many of them are, of course, already birdwatchers, but many are not. Families, children of all ages, people who are simply curious to find out what this birdwatching thing is all about, are all guaranteed a fun and fascinating time. Moreover, I am absolutely certain that they are amazed at the scale of the event.

Above: *Rutland Bird Fair. As you can see from the signposts,*
there's a lot of events: there's bound to be something for everyone.

THE BIRD FAIR

So what is the Bird Fair? It is a cross between a trade fair, an exhibition and a festival. I think of it also as a celebration. Every possible aspect of birds and birding is on display at stands or stalls. You can try out every binocular, telescope and item of photographic gear on the market; browse through every book; try on every type of outdoor clothing; sample the DVDs, CD-ROMs, computer programmes and audio disks. In the art tent, many of the world's top wildlife illustrators display their work and, indeed, are actually painting, sculpting or wood carving before your very eyes. Travel companies from Britain and abroad are represented, as are conservation groups from a variety of countries. You can make your purchases there and then, everything from a painting, to a new binocular strap, to a three-week cruise round the Antarctic.

But it's not just about selling and buying. There is an overflowing programme of illustrated talks, lectures, demonstrations and bird-related activities for youngsters, plus fashion shows, panel games and quizzes, some of which are fairly serious, while others are extremely frivolous. There is good food, live music, and – when you feel like a break – there is excellent birdwatching on the reserve itself. Frankly, it is impossible for me to conjure up what a truly fantastic event this is. I have attended (well, been frantically involved in actually) all but one Rutland Bird Fair since its inception and they just get bigger and better. Unreservedly, I recommend you go.

But what if you are not able to get to Rutland on the third weekend of August? Don't fret. Happily, the success of Rutland has encouraged many other – admittedly smaller – but still hugely entertaining events in various parts of the country. There is a regular Birdwatching and Photographic Fair in July in the Midlands, and others in other areas of Britain. I also hear of more and more in other countries from Poland to the USA. So, wherever you live, at some point in the year, chances are you will have the opportunity to get along to a Bird Fair not too far away.

AND THERE'S MORE

Also, the big conservation organizations frequently hold open days at their most popular reserves or centres, which in many ways are like mini Bird Fairs, again featuring birding products, talks, guided walks and so on.

I have mentioned the benefits of guided group birding. In fact, the RSPB and the Wildlife Trusts hold all sorts of events, which focus more specifically on particular aspects of birds or birding. For example, dawn chorus days, winter wildfowl identification, high tide wader watches, spring migrant specials, and so on and so forth. They really are terrific value, and many of them are so popular that they get booked out well in advance. Members of all such societies will get detailed programmes of events, which go on throughout the year. I cannot stress too strongly that by joining you are not only helping conservation, you are also helping yourself. You get an awful lot back in return.

AND FINALLY ...

I have been a birdwatcher for the last 60 years. Proof in itself that potentially this is a hobby for life. During this time, the technology has changed and improved and so have the related peripherals such as bird art and photography, which are not only impressive in themselves, but have also meant that books and magazines have got better and better. So too has optical equipment. It has also got more and more expensive, to the point that I wonder if the prices are becoming prohibitive.

At least we can take some heart from the fact that the essential gear I needed to become a 'proper birder' back in the 1950's is basically the same today: binoculars, a notebook and pencil, and a field guide. Next phase: save up for a telescope, or don't be shy to ask for a peek through someone else's. Telescopes –spotting scopes, 'scopes – seem to still be evolving and constantly improving. So too of course are websites, -which didn't even exist until relatively recently- along with everything else the Internet has to offer. Which is a lot!

In fact, I doubt that there is a group of people who use the internet more widely than birdwatchers. Research, facts, information, recommendations, where, when and how to watch birds, in Britain and worldwide, and 'recent reports' ,more recent than they have ever been before .It wont be long before we get rarity previews! Frankly, anything and everything bird wise is there somewhere. It is all impressive and entertaining, but the stuff that really excites me is the natural drama ,as on the BTO site following "tagged" Cuckoos to the Congo and back, and the "campaigns"

combating the ever escalating threats to birds and other wildlife,which demonstrate the positive power of Twitter ,rather than the bite size gossip that the name implies. Actually, be fair, anything called Twitter surely ought to belong to the birds? And birdwatchers!

Technology and techniques will change. The appeal of birds wont. Birdwatching can be whatever you want it to be: feeding birds in the garden, twitching, local patch watching, a holiday pursuit, or an occasional distraction. It really doesn't matter. Don't judge yourself, or worry about being judged by others. Enjoy, on whatever level feels right for you. Oh, and whilst you are at it, don't ignore the rest of the natural world: insects, animals, wildflowers, marine life etc. Oh yes, and people. We are all in it together!

Right: *Barn owl – can look like something from outer space! I don't find sitting and surfing on the net as thrilling as seeing a spectacular bird like this out in the open.*

FURTHER INFORMATION

There has never been an easier time to get information on birdwatching (or information on anything actually I suppose). It is strange for me to think back to the time when I first started birding as an early teenager, when the only ID book available was the *Observer's Book of Birds*. It was a nice little book (still in print I believe) but it only had about 40 species in it. Similarly, for many years the only bird magazine available was *British Birds* (happily, still going strong), which – let's face it – was and still is definitely for 'real birdwatchers'. Nowadays, you have a choice of several excellent magazines suitable for varying levels of expertise, all with high quality artwork, news and articles, and masses of adverts for optical equipment, outdoor clothing, books, videos, holidays, etc. I do very strongly recommend that you subscribe to at least one of these magazines and do contact or visit the specialist dealers for whatever you happen to be after. These companies are almost invariably run by birdwatchers for birdwatchers, and you will benefit from honest expert advice.

Of course, over the past decade or two the birding world has been revolutionised by the development of countless birding websites Here are just a few of the many birding websites; only by visiting them will you discover which ones really interest you. Certainly, if you become enticed by twitching and want rare bird news, you will want to visit the relevant sites and phone local or national birdlines. The services they provide are excellent, with news of rare birds updated several times a day.

National Conservation Organizations

Wildfowl & Wetlands Trust
WWT Slimbridge
Gloucestershire GL2 7BT
Tel: 0870 334 4000
www.wwt.org.uk

Royal Society for the Protection of Birds (RSPB) (and Wildlife Explorers)
The Lodge, Sandy
Bedfordshire SG19 2DL
Tel: 01767 680 551
www.rspb.org.uk

The Wildlife Trusts (and Wildlife Watch)
The Kiln, Waterside
Mather Road, Newark
Nottinghamshire NG24 1WT
Tel: 0870 036 7711
www.wildlifetrusts.org

British Trust for Ornithology (BTO)
The Nunnery, Thetford
Norfolk IP24 2PU
Tel: 01842 750 050
www.bto.org

Printed magazines

British Birds
4 Harlequin Gardens,
St Leonards on Sea,
East Sussex TN37 7PF
www.britishbirds.co.uk

Bird Watching
Emap-Active Ltd
Bretton Court
Peterborough PE3 8DZ
www.birdwatching.co.uk

Birdwatch
Warners
West Street, Bourne
Lincolnshire PE10 9PH
www.birdwatch.co.uk

Birds of Britain
(online magazine)
www.birdsofbritain.co.uk

Birding World
Stonerunner, Coast Road
Cley next the Sea, Holt
Norfolk NR25 7RY
www.birdingworld.co.uk

Online shopping: bird books, bird food, etc.

Amazon
www.amazon.co.uk

BirdGuides – www.bird-guides.com

Bird On!
www.birdcare.com/birdon

CJ Wildlife
www.birdfood.co.uk

Ernest Charles
www.ernest-charles.com

Garden Bird Supplies
www.gardenbird.com

Haiths
www.haiths.com

Jacobi Jayne
www.jacobijayne.co.uk

Rob Harvey Specialist Feeds
www.robharvey.com

Other bird-related websites

Fatbirder
www.fatbirder.com

Surfbirds
www.surfbirds.com

Bird links to the world
http://avibase.bsc-eoc.org

Birding UK
www.birding.uk.com

The British Library National Sound Archive
www.bl.uk/listentonature

Bird Fair
www.birdfair.org.uk

Birding For All
(formerly the Disabled Birders Association)
www.birdingforall.com

GLOSSARY

Axillaries: Underwing feathers at the base of the wing forming the so-called 'armpits'.

Coverts: Feathers on the upper and lower surfaces of the wing that assist streamlining in flight.

Eye-stripe: Tract of feathers that runs through the eye.

Flight feathers: Feathers used for flight; the outer primaries and the inner secondaries of the wings.

Irruption: Mass movement of a population from one area to another, usually in response to the exhaustion of food supply. Waxwings are a good example.

Juvenile: A young bird in its full plumage.

Lek: Communal display area used by males of certain species such as Black Grouse and Ruff.

Mantle: The feathers on the back.

Migration: The movement by some species from one area to another, such as Swallows from their wintering grounds in southern Africa to breeding grounds in Europe.

Moult: Because feathers become worn and damaged, they are shed regularly and replaced by new ones.

Passage migrant: A migrant bird that is seen when it stops off to rest and feed while migrating from its breeding grounds to its wintering quarters.

Passerine: A large and extensive group of birds with the ability to perch.

Pelagics: Oceanic seawatching trips usually involving boat.

Plumes: Long, showy feathers often acquired at the start of the breeding season and used for display, such as those shown by egrets.

Race: Distinctive populations of the same species which are usually isolated geographically and show visible, albeit often subtle, plumage differences.

Raptor: Diurnal birds of prey.

Resident: Present within an area throughout the year, such as the Robin.

Species: Genetically distinct individuals, which can breed together and produce viable offspring. However, many species can interbreed and produce viable hybrids, especially ducks.

Speculum: Shiny area of feathering on the secondary flight feathers of many ducks.

Summer plumage: The plumage acquired at the start of the breeding season.

Supercilium: The tract of feathers that runs above the eye and eye-stripe as a distinct stripe, such as that shown by the Sedge Warbler.

Tube-noses: A group of seabirds, with distinctive nostrils, including petrels, shearwaters and fulmars, the last being capable of discharging a pungent, oily substance.

Wader: A group of birds with long legs and bills, often found around the shoreline, including sandpipers, plovers and curlews.

Wildfowl: The family of birds comprising swans, geese and ducks.

Wingspan: The distance between wingtips when fully stretched in flight.

Winter plumage: The plumage seen during the non-breeding winter months.

OTHER BIRD AND WILDLIFE BOOKS BY NEW HOLLAND

Advanced Bird ID Handbook:
The Western Palearctic
Nils van Duivendijk. Award-winning
and innovative field guide covering key
features of every important plumage of all
1,350 species and subspecies that have ever
occurred in Britain, Europe, North Africa
and the Middle East. Published in
association with the journal *British Birds*.
£24.99 ISBN 978 1 78009 022 1
(Also available: *Advanced Bird ID Guide:*
The Western Palearctic £14.99
ISBN 978 1 84773 607 9)

Birds: Magic Moments
Markus Varesvuo. This award-winning
title is a collection of breathtaking
photographs that records fleeting moments
of drama and beauty in the everyday lives
of birds, and allows us all to enter into this
exciting and vibrant world.
£20 ISBN 978 1 78009 075 7
(Also available: *Fascinating Birds*
£20 ISBN 978 1 78009 178 5)

Bill Oddie's Birds of Britain and Ireland
Bill Oddie. New edition of a
comprehensive field guide to more than
200 species of birds, written in the author's
own inimitable style and illustrated with
superb colour artworks by top bird artists.
£12.99 ISBN 978 1 78009 245 4

Bird Songs and Calls
Hannu Jannes and Owen Roberts.
CD with the songs and calls of 96 common
British bird species, accompanied by a book
giving written details and colour photos of
each one. Ideal for learning bird sounds, or
for the dawn chorus season.
£9.99 ISBN 978 1 84773 779 3
(Also available: *Woodland Bird Songs and*
Calls £12.99 ISBN 978 1 78009 248 5;
Wetland Bird Songs and Calls £12.99
ISBN 978 1 78009 249 2)

Chris Packham's Back Garden
Nature Reserve
Chris Packham. A complete guide
explaining the best ways to attract wildlife
into your garden, and how to encourage
it to stay there. Packed with practical
advice on gardening for wildlife and the
identification of birds, animals and plants.
£12.99 ISBN 978 1 84773 698 7

Creative Bird Photography
Bill Coster. Illustrated with the author's
inspirational images. An indispensable
guide to all aspects of the subject, covering
portraits, activities such as courtship, and
taking shots at dawn and dusk.
£14.99 ISBN 978 1 78009 447 2
(Also available: *Creative Nature Photography*
£19.99 ISBN 978 1 84773 784 7)

A Field Guide to the Carnivores of the World

Luke Hunter and Priscilla Barrett. Comprehensive guide to the world's carnivorous mammals. Covers 245 species and includes 86 colour artwork plates plus many line drawings of skulls and footprints.
£24.99 ISBN 978 1 84773 346 7

The Mating Lives of Birds

James Parry. Bird courtship and display is one of the most spectacular events in the natural world. This beautiful book examines everything from territories and song to displays and raising young.
£19.99 ISBN 978 1 84773 937 7

The Naturalized Animals of Britain and Ireland

Christopher Lever. Authoritative and eminently readable account of how alien species were introduced and naturalized, their status and distribution, and their impact. Includes everything from the Ruddy Duck to the Red-necked Wallaby.
£35.00 ISBN 978 1 84773 454 9

New Holland Concise Guides

Ideal first field guides to British wildlife for adults and children. Each covers between 150-300 species in full colour, contains up to 800 colour artworks, comes in protective plastic wallet and includes a fold-out insert comparing species. Series published in association with The Wildlife Trusts.

Titles in the Concise Guide series are as follows (all £4.99):

- *Bird* (ISBN 978 1 84773 601 7)
- *Butterfly & Moth* (ISBN 978 1 84773 602 4)
- *Garden Bird* (ISBN 978 1 84773 978 0)
- *Garden Wildlife* (ISBN 978 1 84773 606 2)
- *Herb* (ISBN 978 1 84773 976 6)
- *Insect* (ISBN 978 1 84773 604 8)
- *Mushroom* (ISBN 978 1 84773 785 4)
- *Pond Wildlife* (ISBN 978 1 84773 977 3)
- *Seashore Wildlife* (ISBN 978 1 84773 786 1)
- *Tree* (ISBN 978 1 84773 605 5)
- *Wild Flower* (ISBN 978 1 84773 603 1)

New Holland European Bird Guide

Peter H Barthel and Paschalis Dougalis. The only truly pocket-sized comprehensive field guide to all the continent's birds. Features more than 1,700 stunning artworks of over 500 species, plus more than 500 distribution maps and a chapter on recognising bird sounds.
£10.99 ISBN 978 1 84773 110 4

Nick Baker's Bug Book

Nick Baker. A fascinating insight into the world of the mini-beast. Includes tips on how to study, identify and attract them to your garden.
£9.99 ISBN 978 1 84773 522 5

Pelagic Birds of the North Atlantic: an ID Guide

Andy Paterson. Innovative new guide, printed on waterproof paper, gives annotated illustrations of every plumage of every pelagic species which could be encountered in the North Atlantic.
£9.99 ISBN 978 1 78009 228 7

Penguins: Close Encounters
David Tipling. The vibrant and exciting world of penguins is shown in all its glory using 140 images by one of the world's top wildlife photographers. Covers all aspects of their life and behaviour and includes all of the world's penguin species.
£20 ISBN 978 1 78009 247 8

Peregrine Falcon
Patrick Stirling-Aird. Beautifully illustrated book detailing the life of this remarkable raptor, including hunting, courtship and raising young. Contains more than 80 stunning colour photographs.
£14.99 ISBN 978 1 84773 769 4
(Also available: *Kingfisher* £12.99 ISBN 978 1 84773 524 9; *Barn Owl* £14.99 ISBN 978 1 84773 768 7)

The Profit of Birding
Bryan Bland. The author is one of birding's greatest story-tellers, and birders and non-birders alike will enjoy the humorous anecdotal narrative, which is accompanied by many of the author's exquisite line-drawings.
£14.99 ISBN 978 1 78009 124 2

Steve Backshall's Deadly 60
Steve Backshall. Join the author on his most daring adventure yet. Best-selling title which accompanies the popular BBC TV series *Deadly 60*.
£9.99 ISBN 978 1 84773 430 3
(Also available:
Steve Backshall's Most Poisonous Creatures
£9.99 ISBN 978 1 78009 462 5)

Steve Backshall's Wildlife Adventurer's Guide
Steve Backshall. With Britain's leading adventure naturalist as your guide, you'll be inspired to discover the joys of wildlife while experiencing the thrill of exploring.
£14.99 ISBN 978 1 84773 324 5

Tales of a Tabloid Twitcher
Stuart Winter. Britain's only tabloid journalist birder covers all the key events and personalities of the past two decades and beyond, from David Attenborough to 'Sammy the Stilt'.
£7.99 ISBN 978 1 84773 693 2
(Also available: *The Birdman Abroad* £7.99 ISBN 978 1 84773 692 5)

Top 100 Birding Sites of the World
Dominic Couzens. An inspiration for the travelling birder. Brings together a selection of the best places to go birdwatching on Earth, from Norfolk to New Zealand, covering every continent. Includes 350 photos and more than 100 maps.
£19.99 ISBN 978 1 78009 460 1

The Urban Birder
David Lindo. Even the most unpromising cityscapes can be great for birds. Popular TV personality, magazine columnist and blogger David Lindo's very readable book includes tales of gun-toting youths and migration-watching from skyscrapers.
£9.99 ISBN 978 1 78009 494 6

See www.newhollandpublishers.com for details and special offers

INDEX

Page numbers in **bold** refer to illustrations